SYLLABUS

OF

Lectures on Civil Engineering,

IN THE

UNIVERSITY OF GEORGIA.

BY CHARLES F. McCAY,

Prof. of Mathematics and Civil Engineering.

Athens, Ga.
CHRISTY & KELSEA.
1853.

ERRATA.

Page 4,	line 34,	for England had 10000,	read England had 30000,
11,	" 29,	" less,	" loss.
14,	" 9,	" 4 to 3,	" 3 to 4.
17,	" 38,	" $(H \div S-f)$	" $(H \div S-f)$.
29,	" 30,	" $2\frac{2}{3}^2$,	" $2\frac{1}{2}^2$.
29,	" 35,	" $\frac{1}{270}$,	" $\frac{1}{720}$.
36,	" 14,	after per ton,	add per hundred miles.
37,	" 3,	" 50cts,	" per ton.
41,	" 1,	for feet,	read inches.
44,	" 37,	" 13007,	" 13006.
45,	" 1,	" 8118,	" 9118.
54,	" 8,	" any,	" an.
60,	" 36,	after friction,	add for.
61,	" 4,	" tolls,	" estimating the cost of a horse at 50cts per day.
61,	" 10,	" profitable,	" in the South.
68,	" 5,	" Oglethorpe,	" Columbus.
73,	" 16,	" track,	" of the curves.
80,	" 14,	for only double,	read equal to.
80,	" 25,	" dense,	" close.
104,	" 33,	after parallel,	add and equal.
108,	" 24,	for line,	read sine.
109,	" 15,	" $\frac{3}{1}$	" $\frac{3}{10}$.
109,	" 16,	" 916.5,	" 916.6.
111,	" 19,	" 16 DB,	" 16.′ BD.
111,	" 28,	" treverse,	" reverse.
112,	" 7,	" $\frac{7}{8}cd$,	" $\frac{7}{8}cd^2$.
112,	" 29,	" 43′,	" 45′.
112,	" 32,	" $200\frac{1}{2}$,	" $202\frac{1}{2}$.
112,	" 37,	" $x \div a$,	" $x+a$.
113,	" 8,	" $\frac{7}{8}n^2c$,	" $\frac{7}{8}x^2c$.
118,	" 26,	" 30	" 30.

LECTURE I.

INTRODUCTION.

1. *The duties of the Civil Engineer are numerous and important.*

Along the sea, he builds sea-walls to protect the shore from being worn away by the waves; dry docks and floating docks, to receive ships for examination and repairs; light-houses, where they are exposed to the violence of the ocean; and break-waters, to form an artificial harbor in which ships may ride in safety, when a storm is raging without.

Along rivers, he constructs bridges of wood, stone or iron, when the stream is wide, and the piers exposed to uncommon injuries; aqueducts, where a large channel of water is to be conducted over a valley or a river; locks, or chambers into which loaded boats are to be floated and raised or lowered from one level to another; and dams, where the stream is wide, or deep, or rapid, or the structure exposed to damage from violent floods, or large masses of floating ice.

On land, he digs tunnels through hills or mountains, he sinks Artesian wells one or two thousand feet deep, and builds those massive machines or structures which require great strength and superior mechanical skill in their construction.

He lays out common roads, turn-pikes, plank-roads, and railways, and prepares them for the transportation of merchandise; removes the obstructions from rivers, deepens their channels, and makes them navigable in one or both directions; and digs canals or artificial channels in which boats or ships may be transported from one place to another.

In all these works, he selects the materials, as to their kind, quality, cost, and amount; measures the earth-work, timber, masonry, and carpentry; decides when all is done in a workmanlike manner; and superintends every operation, from the first breaking of the ground to the final completion of the work, so as to be responsible for the manner in which the whole is executed.

2. *To perform these duties properly requires a thorough knowledge of science.*

To lay out his roads and canals, he must be acquainted with Geometry, Surveying, and Levelling; to measure his materials and work, he must understand Mensuration; and in finding the solidity and areas of irregular figures, in discussing the chain-curve for suspension bridges, in determining the forms of arches, the principles of Algebra and the Calculus will be necessary.

To lay out his railways and canals with proper skill, he must be familiar with the laws of the inclined plane and of water, of inertia gravity and friction, and of momentum velocity and force. In all his structures he must understand the composition and resolution of forces, and the influence of form, length, depth and breadth on the strength of materials. The principles of the mechanical powers, and in fact, every department of mechanics and hydrostatics will be of advantage to him.

In his tunnels and excavations, a knowledge of Geology will be useful; in his selection of materials, Mineralogy, Chemistry and Botany will be of service; and in determining the style and character of his work and in arranging the tariff of tolls, the principles of Political Economy will furnish assistance.

3. *In all these sciences his knowledge must not only be theoretical but practical.*

In his mathematical calculations, he will often use approximate methods instead of the more laborious but exact rules of the science. He must make the usual deductions and allowances, which can only be learned from the local or general customs of the trades. In natural philosophy the laws of the lever and inclined plane, are commonly studied without reference to friction and other resistances; but in practice these things must be considered, as they seriously affect the results. The strength and elasticity of materials, their cost and durability, their suitableness for a particular work, the injuries to which they are exposed from violent blows, from continued wear and tear, from the action of air, rain, resistance, heat, frost, earth and water, can only be learned in the school of experience.

4. *Of these duties, the subject of Roads and Canals and the improvement of rivers are selected for our study.*

Because all would occupy more time than we can spare, because these subjects are more likely to be useful to all of us, are closely connected with our College studies, and can be pursued without models and without an ocular inspection of the works that have been constructed.

5. *This subject claims your interest and attention, because of the utility of good roads.*

Good roads are useful, because the diversity of soil and climate in different parts of the world enable the agriculturist to produce an article at much less cost snd labor at one place than another, and good roads enable the consumer to obtain this product at a slight addition to the cost of production at the cheapest place.

Again, mines of coal, iron, lead, copper, salt, and other articles are found only in particular places, and the price to the consumer being dependent on the cost of mining and of transportation, good roads, by lessening this last element of cost reduce the charge to the consumer.

This same advantage is felt, when extensive water power or cheap fuel at one place enables a manufacturer to produce an article at a low cost ; or when all the elements necessary to a particular production are found in juxtaposition ; as when the iron ore, the limestone, the fuel and the water power, needed in the manufacture of iron, are all found in close proximity.

Besides, good roads are necessary to a proprer division of labor. This division cheapens very much the cost of articles, but in order to effect it, an extensive production is necessary. As these numerous products cannot be consumed in the immediate vicinity, they must be transported to a distance, and without good roads to lessen the cost of carriage, the advantages of the division of labor would be lost.

Good roads increase very much the value of land, by bringing, as it were, the most distant places near to market. A valley of the richest land two or three hundred miles from a market is almost worthless without good roads, but the opening of a railway might make this land worth twenty or thirty, or perhaps fifty dollars per acre. This is especially true when the product is heavy in proportion to its value, as corn or oats, or even wheat.

The benefits of good roads are felt, both by the producer and the consumer, by the farmer and the resident of the city. The former buys his salt, iron, coffee and sugar cheaper than before, and sells his cotton, tobacco, corn and wheat for a higher price. The latter enlarges his commercial transactions on account of the increased demand at lower prices, and supplies his table with the products of the country at cheaper rates. The saving in transportation is thus divided by both parties.

Improved roads not only cheapen products, but save the time of the man of business ; increase the safety and comfort of travellers, and enlarge their number ; and by facilitating commerce and social intercourse, add to the civilization refinement and happiness of society.

6. *This subject farther claims attention, because of the magnitude and importance of these Internal Improvements in our own and other countries.*

In the United States, besides the sums expended on common roads, not less than eight hundred millions of dollars have been expended on our canals and slack-water navigation, turnpikes, and railroads. At the beginning of 1853, we had 4000 miles of canals, 1000 miles of slack-water navigation, 10000 miles of turnpike roads, and 13000 miles of railways. England had 10000 miles of turnpikes, 3000 of canals, and 7000 of railways. These have cost her eighteen hundred millions of dollars. On the continent of Europe, there are 9000 miles of railways, which have cost seven hundred millions. Nearly all these railroads have been built since 1830, and the progress, which they are everywhere making, warrants us in expecting that in less than ten years the number of miles will be doubled. An interest so immense, controlled and managed by science, is worthy of our attention and study.

7. *This subject farther claims attention, because most of our State Governments are interested in these Improvements.*

Many political questions necessarily arise on account of this interest. The propriety of beginning new works, of disposing of those already built, of aiding and encouraging others by subscriptions to the stock, or endorsements of the bonds, by loans, gifts, charters, privileges, freedom from taxation, must often be discussed ; and in our republican country all of us may be called on to give our vote in the decision of these questions.

8. *This subject is well suited for college study, since it unites mental improvement with practical utility.*

The main object of education is, indeed, to develope in full and perfect proportion, all the powers of the mind ; to improve the memory ; to cultivate the imagination ; to strengthen the reasoniug powers ; to accustom the intellect to all kinds of exercise, both in the regions of probable and demonstrative evidence ; to form habits of attention, discrimination, acuteness and accuracy ; to awaken the love of truth, of science and of nature ; and to make us acquainted with the profound wisdom every where displayed in the works of creation. But, if while cultivating the mental faculties, the useful and practical can also be pursued, they should not be neglected. The study of Civil Engineering combines both these objects. While we shall at all times attend to the proof of the propositions advanced, we shall be learning truths that will be of use to us in after life ; so that while the intellect is exercised, the mind will be stored with useful knowledge.

LECTURE II.

GRAVITY.

9. *The object of the Engineer, in constructing his roads and canals, is to reduce the resistances in Transportation, to accommodate these to the powers at his command, and to effect these objects in as cheap and durable a manner as possible.*

Some of these resistances can be lessened, as friction, obstacles, air, and water; some cannot, as gravity and inertia. Some can be reduced considerably at a slight expense. Some almost annihilated, but at a great sacrifice of time and money. Some can be so divided and distributed that only a small portion is to be overcome at each instant. And the object of the Engineer is to reduce and adjust the magnitude of each resistance, that at every instant it may be so suited to the power he is using, that the whole resistance may be overcome, to the greatest advantage and at the smallest expense.

10. *The powers of the Engineer are steam, the force of animals, gravity and water-power. The resistances are gravity, friction, obstacles, inertia, air and water.*

Some of these are included under both heads; as gravity on a descending river or on an inclined plane is at one time a power and at another a resistance. Water-power derives its energy from gravity, but it will be best to treat it separately.

11. *These powers and resistances are all measured by a common standard, and this is the momentum of a given weight raised vertically with a given velocity.*

Unless all are measured by a common standard, it is impossible to compare them one with another, to estimate their joint effect when acting together or opposing each other, and to adapt the resistance to the powers employed in overcoming them.

There are two measures of force, one the distance it moves a body in the unit of time, and the other the momentum it gives. When the earth draws the moon a certain distance towards it, sometimes the space is regarded as the measure of the earth's influence, and sometimes the product of the space into the mass of the moon. The former is sometimes called acting force, the latter moving force. It is this last that we shall reckon as power or as force in Engineering. Our force is a momentum, a product arising from multiplying a weight into its velocity.

A road or canal is made for transportation ; a weight is to be moved from one place to another; and the resistance to be considered, and the force to overcome that resistance is always a momentum. When a wagon is drawn by a horse on a level or on an inclined plane, we may imagine the wagon to be removed, and a rope attached to the horse and extended horizontally over a pulley, and a weight of such a size fastened to the rope, that the horse must exert the same force to raise the weight as he did to pull the wagon. Then not the weight, but the momentum of the weight will measure the resistance caused by the wagon, and also the force exerted by the horse. If a load of 1000 lbs. is moved at three miles per hour, and the effort of the horse at A (fig. 1) is the same as if he were raising a weight of 60 lbs. at C, attached to the rope ABC passing horizontally over a pulley at B, then the force of the horse or the resistance of the load is measured by 3 X 60 lbs. So with the power of steam. The piston, moving under a pressure on each inch of its surface, may be regarded as a weight moving with a certain velocity, and its momentum is the measure of its power. So are all powers and all resistances regarded as equal to the momentum of a weight moving vertically with some particular velocity.

By force then we understand moving force, or the product obtained by multiplying a weight into its velocity ; and we measure all powers and all resistances by this standard.

12. ***When a loaded car is on an inclined plane, the ten-***

dency to descend, on account of gravity, is measured by multiplying the weight into the height of the plane and dividing by the length.

This may be proved by the resolution of forces. Thus, if weight on the inclined plane AC, (fig. 2) be represented by DE, and DE be resolved into the two weights, DF and DG, one along AC and the other perpendicular to AC, DF measures the whole tendency to descend. And by similar triangles ABC and DEF

AC:CB::DE:DF, or,

DF=whole weight DE X height CB and divided by length AC, or=WH÷L; if W H and L represent the weight and the height and the length of the plane.

Again, this may be proved by experiment; if a set of wheels weighing W rest on AC, and be sustained by a weight P suspended from a string passing over a pulley at C and fastened to the wheels, it is found by experiment that P=WH÷L.

13. *The moving force required to draw a body on an inclined plane is the product of WH÷ L into V, if V represent the velocity at which the body is moved.*

For in the experiment just referred to, P will not only balance WH÷L at rest, but will keep it moving uniformly if in motion. Now the momentum of P is PV, which is equal to WHV÷ L. The momentum of P is its power or moving force. Therefore, the moving force required to draw W on the inclined plane with a velocity of V is WHV÷ L.

14. *The force required to move a load on an inclined plane varies as the load, and as the velocity, and as the height of the plane divided by the length.*

This follows from the formula F=WHV÷ L. With twice the load, or twice the velocity, or twice the rise in a mile, the force required is doubled.

15. *The whole work done in any time is measured by the product of the moving force and the time during which the force is exerted; that is, if T represent the time, the work done is WVT.*

Thus the *work done* by a horse drawing a weight out of

a well by a rope attached, is the weight X its velocity X the time the horse is at work. If the weight is 100 lbs. and the velocity 3 feet per second, and the horse work 8 hours, the *work done* is $100 \times 3 \times 8 \times 60 \times 60$, or 100 lbs. raised 86400 feet. If 1200 lbs. is drawn up a hill rising one foot in height to ten in length, with a velocity of two miles per hour, and the horse works 7 hours, the work done is $1200 \times \frac{1}{10} \times 2 \times 7$ or 120 lbs. raised vertically 14 miles; because the moving force is $WHV \div L$ or $1200 \times \frac{1}{10} \times 2$, and the time is 7 hours.

16. *The work done in drawing a body up the whole length of an inclined plane is independent of the velocity.*

If the velocity of the moving body is doubled, the moving force must be doubled. But the time during which that increased force must be exerted to carry the body to the top of the plane must be halved, so that the product of the moving force into the time is unchanged.

17. *The work done in drawing a body up an inclined plane is the same as in lifting it vertically through the height of the plane.*

Because the moving force required on the plane is $WHV \div L$ and the whole work of drawing it up is $WHVT \div L$, if T is the time. But $VT = L$; therefore, by substitution, the whole whole work is $WHL \div L$ or WH.

Again, the moving force required to lift W vertically is WV. The work done is WVT, if T is the time of lifting it. But now $VT = H$; hence, by substitution the work done is WH, which is the same as on the inclined plane.

18. *The moving force required to move a body over a level plane is nothing.*

Because, the power is represented by $WHV \div L$, and if H is zero, this product becomes zero.

19. *The moving force expended in transporting a body between two points that are on the same level is zero, whatever be the route between the points.*

For if the route descends first and then rises afterwards, as in (fig. 3,) the momentum generated in falling through AB will carry the body up to C, if A and C are on the same level.

If the route rises first and then descends as in ADC, some force must be exerted to raise the body up to D; but in descending through DC the final momentum acquired will be sufficient to raise the body as high as D; so that the force retained at C equals the force expended on AD, and none is therefore lost. In a similar manner this could be proved, if the plane were undulating, rising and falling several times, as in AEFGC.

20. *The whole work done in transporting a body from one point to another, whatever be the route, is the same as if the body is lifted vertically through a space equal to the height of the second point above the first.*

For the whole work done in drawing a body up one plane is (by 17) the same as in lifting the body through its height; and this is true for any number of planes. If some of the planes descend, the momentnm gained in falling down these will carry the body up the same height on the next ascending plane, so that the excess of the height of the second plane above the first is all that is to be overcome.

21. *The whole resistance offered by gravity between two given points can in no way be reduced or annihilated.*

Whether the route be a regular ascent, long or short, undulating with slight ascents or descents, rising or falling suddenly and steeply, the resistance is the same. No effort of the Engineer can lessen or alter the whole force that must be expended to transport a body between the two points. But still,

22. *A good road must avoid all steep ascents, so that the motive power may produce the greatest useful effect.*

For if the horse were loaded to his full average power on the level, he would be either unable to draw his load up the steep ascents, or he would be strained or injured by the effort. If his load were limited to what he can draw on the ascents, he is underworked on the level part of the road, and the time of the horse and of the attendants, and the wear and tear of the wagon and harness will be expended to but little purpose.

By making the rise at each moment small, and thus distributing the whole force of gravity over a long space, the total resistance to be overcome is not lessened; but the amount for each instant adds but a trifle to the friction, so that the joint effect of the two resistances is kept all the while nearly the same, and the horse can draw nearly his full load on the level.

So with the locomotive. Its efficiency will be greater, on a road with gentle ascents, than when the grade is steep for a short distance and then level or undulating for the greater portion of the way.

23. *Steep ascents must be avoided for another reason. The loss in ascending them cannot be balanced by the gain in descending.*

For if gravity be permitted to act on the descents with its full force, the vehicle would move down with a dangerous rapidity. As the brake must be applied on the railway, and the horse compelled to hold back on the common road, there is an expenditure of force, both in ascending and in descending, making thus a double loss instead of a compensation for the first.

24. *Undulating roads, where the ascents and descents are not so great that the wagon or car would run down by gravity alone, are nearly as good as level roads.*

For none of the objections to steep ascents apply to these roads. A horse or a locomotive can do, without injury, a little more work at one time than another; and they can do this all day, about to the same advantage as if required to exert a moderate uniform force for the whole time; there is no less of momentum on the descents; and the load can be nearly as large as if the road were level.

25. *A level road, whether for a horse or a locomotive, is the best of all, and among undulating roads, the nearer to being level the better.*

The load may be greater on a level road than on any other, and every increase in the ascent diminishes the amount of the load.

When horses are used, their efficiency on undulating roads is less than on a level, on account of the force required to raise the horse's body up the ascents. It is easier for a horse or a man to go down a slight declivity than to move on a perfect level, but it is not much easier. Whereas to ascend an acclivity is much more difficult than to go on a level. The loss in ascending is thus not made up by the gain in descending. The two are balanced in a rolling body, as a wagon, but not with a walking one, as a man or a horse.

It is sometimes said that a horse uses different muscles in going up and going down hills, and thus the change is a kind of rest to him. This can hardly apply when the road merely undulates, so that he has to pull all the while. The only change he then has, is between pulling much and little. The same muscles are employed, the strain on them being the only thing variable. And this gives no preference to undulating roads over level ones.

LECTURE III.

FRICTION.

26. *The friction at the circumference of the wheel is variable and uncertain.*

It is very large on soft muddy roads, especially when the soil is stiff or tough. If the way is dry and hard, this friction is very slight. On good railways it is almost nothing.

Sometimes the rubbing of the flanges or guides on the wheels, against the rails, may produce a large resistance on railroads, especially on curves; but this is prevented or lessened by giving a conical shape to the wheels, the larger diameter being on the inside next to the flange, so as to turn the train away from that side where the wheels are rubbing or about to rub against the rails.

This friction at the rim cannot well be reduced to any laws worthy of our attention. Not so with friction at the axle. This resistance is important everywhere, and its laws are well understood.

27. *The friction at the axle increases as the load.*

If a block be drawn on a smooth level plane, the force required to move this uniformly is found by experiment to be doubled for double weights, and so on, increasing as the weight. The friction, therefore, caused by the pressure of the load on the axle increases as its weight.

Numerous experiments made by Vince and Morin have fully established this and the following law.

28. *Friction is independent of the surface in contact.*

If the same block is drawn on different faces, varying very much in size, the resistance is found by experiment to be the same. It follows from this, that the friction of a car is not affected by the number of the wheels. With two, four, or eight, the rubbing surface at the axle varies, but not the resistance. Nor is the friction dependent on the length or breadth of the surface of contact between the axle and the boxes of the wheels.

29. *The force required to overcome friction increases as the radius of the axle and decreases as the radius of the wheel.*

For the power to turn the wheel around may be regarded as applied at the ground as at B (fig. 4) and pulling backwards from B to A, and the resistance as applid at C the circumference of the axle. The arm or lever on which the power acts is, therefore, BD, while the arm on which the resistance acts is CD. Now, according to the principles of the lever, the longer DC is, the greater is the efficiency of the friction, that is the greater will be the difficulty of overcoming it; and the longer BD is, the easier will this resistance be overcome. Hence the resistance, compared with a fixed power applied at B varies as DC directly and BD inversely, or as $r \div R$, if r and R represent the radii of the axle and of the wheel.

This has also been proved by experiments made by

Tredgold. A small wagon with two sets of wheels was drawn on a plane, at the same velocity, by weights attached to a string passing ovet a pulley, and the weights were found to vary inversely as the radii of the wheels. In like manner was an experiment tried for different axles.

Again, experiments made by Wood showed that with the same fuel and load the distance gone over by a locomotive first with 3 feet wheels and then with 4 feet wheels varied as 4 to 3.

This result might have been expected, for the rubbing surface at the axle being supposed to be dragged through the same space by the same expenditure of force, the distance traversed by the rim of the wheel would increase as the size of the wheel. That is, the effect increases as the radius of the wheel. The same reasoning applied to the axle would show that the effect is inversely as its radius. Hence the effect varies as $\frac{R}{r}$. But the resistance is inversely as the effect, hence the resistance varies as $r \div R$.

30. *Although the wheels should be as large and the axles as small as possible, their size must be suited to the purposes for which they are used.*

On a common road large wheels are objectionable on account of the difficulty of loading, and of turning; and because of their increased weight and cost; and on railroads, because of the elevation of the centre of gravity. This gives a lateral motion to the train, and causes the flanges at the rim of the wheels to rub against the sides of the rails. This friction is very large, because it acts so far from the centre of motion, and because it cannot be lessened by the use of oil or tallow. There is a limit also to the smallness of the axles, as they must be large enough to sustain the load. Iron is thus preferable to wood for axles, because they can then be made smaller.

31. *The resistance from friction, and the moving force necessary to overcome it, increases, at each instant, with the velocity.*

The weight that draws a block forward on a plane with a small velocity, is found by experiment to be able to keep it in motion uniformly at all velocities. Now, the momentum or moving force of this weight increases with the velocity. Therefore, friction increases with the velocity.

The experiments made by Morin, to test this law, were varied from the slowest perceptible motion up to ten feet per second.

32. *The whole work done in a given distance in overcoming friction is independent of the velocity.*

For although the moving force to be exerted at each instant increases with the velocity, yet the time during which this force has to be exerted decreases in the same ratio. So that the whole force expended in transporting a body over, given space is the same whatever be the velocity.

33. *The resistance offered by gravity and friction are in many respects similar.*

Both increase with the velocity at each instant of time, both are independent of velocity for a given distance, both increase with the weight of the load to be moved, both are measured by a weight suspended by a string passing over a pulley, and both are constant forces.

34. *The amount of friction on common hard roads with the usual wheels and unguents is about one twentieth of the load, and on railroads about one two hundred and fortieth of the load.*

That is, on a common road, one pound hung by a rope behind the vehicle, passing over a pulley, exerts the same resistance as 20 placed on the wheels; on a railroad the one pound is equivalent to 240 on the wheels.

These numbers are not exact, but average amounts. On a common road, friction may be as small as $\frac{1}{30}$ sometimes. On a railroad it ranges from 7 lbs. to 11 lbs per ton, that is from $\frac{1}{320}$ to $\frac{1}{204}$; but it is usually about $\frac{1}{240}$.

The reasons of this great difference are the smaller diameters of the axle of the car compared with the load, it being of iron; the superior unguents used on railroads; the regularity with which these are supplied; and the greater smoothness and hardness of the railway.

35. *The simplest mode of determining the amount of friction is by a spring balance.*

If a loaded wagon or car is drawn forward by the intervention of a spring balance between the power and the load, the pounds indicated by the balance become a measure of the friction, if the road is level. Thus, if the load weighed 1000 lbs. and the balance was drawn out 50 lbs., it is evident that if the load were removed and a weight of 50 lbs. attached to a string passing over a pulley and then fastened to the balance by which the horse was pulling, the weight would draw out the balance 50 lbs. So that the weight 50 lbs. produces the same effect as the load, and therefore, measures the friction of the 1000 lbs. In like manner, if the cars on a level railroad were attached to the locomotive by the intervention of a balance, the pounds indicated by the balance would be the friction of the load. Thus, if the load were 15 tons of 2000 lbs. each, and the pounds shown by the balance 100, the friction would be $\frac{1}{300}$ of the load.

If the load were drawn up an inclined plane, the pounds shown by the balance would measure gravity plus friction, and since gravity can be calclated by the formula $\frac{WH}{L}$, the remainder, which is the friction, will be known. Thus, if a car weighs 20 tons of 2000 lbs., and the balance shows 450 lbs., when the plane rises 33 feet in a mile; we must subtract from the whole resistance which is 450 lbs., the gravity which is $20 \times 2000 \times 33 \div 5280$ or 250 lbs., and the remainder 200 lbs. is the friction. The fraction which this is of the whole load is $\frac{1}{200}$.

To get the momentum of this weight, which is the moving force required to overcome friction, we must multiply these pounds by the velocity of the load.

This method of obtaining the friction, though simple, is not very exact, because the vehicle moves forward by irregular jerks, the resistance being variable even on the smoothest roads; and consequently the balance oscillates more or less. The average will be nearly the true resistance but not exactly. On a canal the results are more regular and reliable.

36. *A second method of obtaining the amount of friction is by means of a plane so inclined that a body will remain at rest or descend uniformly.*

On such a plane the gravity is exactly balanced by the friction, and since the former is known the latter is also. Thus, on a common road, if a plane falls about one foot in twenty of its length, it is found by experience, that a wagon will descend without any exertion from the horse either to hold back or pull forward. Hence friction is $\frac{1}{20}$ of the load. On a railway this plane is found to fall about 22 feet in a mile. Friction is then $\frac{WH}{L}$ or 22 W÷ 5280 or 1÷240th of the load on a railroad. This method is not exact in practice, because it is difficult to determine when the body moves uniformly.

37. *A third method of obtaining the amount of friction is by noting the space described in a given time by a car descending an inclined plane from a state of rest.*

By the laws of bodies moving under the influence of a constant force, $S = mFT^2$
where S is the space, m $16\frac{1}{12}$ feet, F the force and T the time. Now, on a descending plane, the force is gravity less friction; or if f be the friction, $F = H \div L - f$ hence $S = m\,(H \div L - f)\,T^2$ or $S \div mT^2 = H \div L - f$ or $f = H \div L - S \div mT^2$.

As an example by this formula; in an experiment made by Wood, the inclination of the plane was 1 yard in 104, and the car descended 939 feet in 108 seconds; then $f = \frac{1}{104} - 939 \div 16\frac{1}{12} \times 11664 = \frac{1}{104} - \frac{1}{200} = \frac{1}{216}$.

This method, though more exact than either of the two preceding, is imperfect, from the difficulty of noting the exact time of starting and stopping; and a slight error in this becomes important, since T is squared.

38. *A fourth method of obtaining the amount of friction, is by having two planes meeting each other, one descending and the other ascending, and noting how far a body will rise on the second after running down the first.*

In this case, the square of the velocity at the bottom of the first $= 4mFS = 4m\,(H \div S - f)\,S = 4m\,(H - fS)$, if m, F, S,

f and H represent $16\frac{1}{12}$ feet, the force, the space fallen through, the friction, and the height, of the plane.

On a second plane, if we represent similar quantities by the same letters accented, the square of the velocity with which the body must be started at the bottom of the plane is $4mF'S'$ or $4m\,(H'\div S'+f)\,S'$ or $4m\,(H'+S'f)$, the friction f being the same as before, and now aiding gravity instead of retarding it, as it did in the descent. But these two velocities are the same; therefore, $4m(H-fS)=4m\,(H'+fS')$ or $H-fS=H'+fS'$ or $f=(H-H')\div(S+S')$.

This formula is very simple, easily employed, and gives very exact results.

As an example, from Wood's experiments, a carriage having run down a plane 1467 feet long, ascended another 1166 feet long, and the difference in the level of the two points was 11.61 feet. Therefore $f=11.61\div 2633=\frac{1}{227}$.

A great number of experiments have been made in this way, and the result of all is that friction on a railway ranges, as was said before, from 7 to 11 lbs. per ton, or on an average it is about $\frac{1}{240}$ of the weight or load.

39. *The force necessary to overcome gravity and friction, which are the principal resistances on railways and common roads is* $(H\div L+f)WV$.

Gravity is on both $WVH\div L$ and friction f on one is $\frac{1}{20}$ WV and on the other $\frac{1}{240}$ WV. Example: On a common road, rising one foot in 12, the friction to be overcome with a load cf 1200 lbs. is 60V. Gravity is $HWV\div L$ or $\frac{1}{12}\times 1200V$ or 100V, and both=160V. That is, the resistance is the same as if 160 lbs. were suspended by a string and raised vertically with a velocity equal to V.

On a railroad rising 11 feet in a mile with a load of 120 tons of 2000 lbs. each, gravity is $120\times 2000\times 11V\div 5280$ or 500 V; friction is $120\times 2000V\div 240$ or 1000V and both =1500V; that is, the resistance is the same as if 1500lbs. were raised vertically with a velocity=V.

LECTURE IV.

INERTIA, OBSTACLES AND THE RESISTANCE OF THE AIR.

40. *Besides gravity and friction, there are three other resistances to be overcome both on a common road and on a railway; these are inertia, obstacles and the resistance of the air.*

These five constitute the whole resistance to be overcome when a body is moved from one place to another.

41. *Inertia is only felt as a resistance when the velocity with which a body moves is changed.*

If the body is at rest, inertia must be overcome to set it in motion; if it is in motion, inertia must be overcome to give it a higher or a lower velocity or to stop it entirely.

42. *Inertia causes no loss of power when the vehicle is stopped without the application of the brake or the holding back of the horse.*

The horse and the steam expended some of their force in starting the body, and in giving it more and more velocity; but the momentum the body thus acquires will carry it forward after the horse or steam has ceased to exert any force, precisely as far as the power which gave the momentum would have done. Thus the power is only loaned, not expended.

Whenever the horse holds back or the brake is applied to the car, then the inertia is taken away and lost. The loss is two-fold, since force is exerted both to give and take away momentum.

43. *On a common road, the force required to overcome inertia is small, and the force lost still less.*

It is small because the load and the velocity are both small. Thus, if a vehicle is to move at the rate of five miles per hour, the inertia might be overcome by making it fall down an inclined plane at starting. Now, on inclined planes, $V^2 = 4mFS = 4mHS \div L = 4mH$, if L be taken equal to S. But if V is 5 miles per hour or $5 \times 5280 \div 3600$ or $7\frac{1}{3}$ feet per second, H is $(7\frac{1}{3})^2 \div 4 \times 16\frac{1}{12}$ or .83 of a foot. That is, the descent down an inclined plane whose height is .83 of a foot would overcome entirely the inertia of the body. The horse must then expend the same force as would raise the body through this height. Now, to raise a body a foot, is the same as to draw it 20 feet forwards on a common level road, overcoming friction only, since friction is $\frac{1}{20}$W. Therefore, the same force must be expended to give a body a velocity of five miles an hour as to carry it on a level through the space of $20 \times .83$ or 16.6 feet.

When a vehicle is stopped it is always done gradually. The friction, therefore, takes away a larger or smaller portion of the inertia. The part taken away by the horse, which is all that is lost, is but a part of the whole. That is, the force lost is but a part of the force required to draw the body on a level through the distance of 16.6 feet.

44. *On a railroad, the force and time required to overcome inertia are considerable, but the force lost is a small part of the whole amount expended, except for trains of high velocities.*

The load and velocity both being large, the inertia is large. If the velocity were 10 miles an hour, the height H through which the body must fall to acquire this velocity is as before$=V^2 \div 4m$. But V is now $14\frac{2}{3}$ feet per second; therefore, $H=3.33$. Therefore, the force required to overcome inertia, is in this case, the same as is required to raise the body through the height of $3\frac{1}{3}$ feet, or to move it on a level the distance of 800 feet. Now, if one-half of this be supposed to be lost by using the brake, and the train stop every five miles, this loss requires that the force expended should be sufficient to move the body 5 miles +400 feet, instead of 5 miles; that is, the whole force required is increased the 66th part, the road being level.

But if the velocity is 30 miles and the stoppages occur every 5 miles, either to get wood or water, or to take in or put off passengers, or for other causes, then the H calculated as before is a trifle more than 30 feet. And the distance, which is equivalent to this height is, if the road be level, 240×30 or 7200 feet, or more than a mile and a third. And if one-half of the inertia is destroyed by the brake, the force to be exerted will be the force necessary to carry the body 5 miles +3600 feet, instead of 5 miles; that is, it is increased about one-seventh.

45. *The resistance from obstacles differs from both friction and gravity.*

It may arise, on a common road, from stones or other obstructions; and on a railway, from the unevenness of the joints of the rails, or from the surface being covered with sand, ashes, or dust of any kind.

46. *If the obstacle yields, or is crushed, as the wheel rises over it, the loss may be considerable.*

On common roads, the sandy road is known to cause a large resistance, although the sand yields before the wheel. And, on railroads, it was found in an experiment of Tredgold, that the force required to draw a car was increased 19 per cent. when the rails were slightly covered with dust.

47. *If the vehicle passes over the obstacle without a shock, the resistance is insensible.*

The body, in this case, may be regarded as moving on a curve, in which it is known there is no loss of velocity from the change of direction.

48. *When the obstacle gives a shock to the vehicle, the injury done is of various kinds.*

It demands force to raise the body over the obstruction, increases the friction, lessens the velocity, injures the cars and locomotive, and gives a jolt to the train, which is unpleasant to the passengers, and often injurious to the freight.

49. *There is no loss of power in lifting the vehicle over the obstacle.*

Force is required to raise the body, but it is fully returned in the descent on the other side of the obstruction. The power is therefore not expended or lost.

50. *The force required to overcome the axle friction is increased in the ratio of R–h to R.*

The absolute resistance produced by the rubbing at the axle is not increased, but the leverage by which it is overcome is lessened, so that greater force must be applied. Thus (fig. 5), the axle friction is at A, and the radius of the wheel CB is ordinarily the lever arm by which the friction is overcome. But when the obstacle EF meets the wheel, the lever arm is CD; the power required must therefore increase, in the ratio of CD to CB, or as R–h to R, if R represent the radius of the wheel and h the height of the obstacle EF.

51. *If the obstacle be large, the increase of force required is considerable; but usually it is slight and unimportant.*

If h=R the vehicle would be stopped entirely. If h=$\frac{3}{4}$R, the force would be increased four fold. But on a railway or a good common road, the obstacles being small compared with the radius, and only increasing the friction for an instant, the additional power demanded by the friction is quite small.

52. *The principal resistance from obstacles arises from the sudden change of direction in the moving body, by which a part of its velocity is lost.*

If a body is moving forward in the line CG, and at C is forced to move in the line CH, the velocity in the new direction is less than before. If CG represent the former velocity and GH be drawn perpendicular to CH, the new velocity will be CH. The former velocity is to the new as radius to the cosine of the angle between the two directions.

This loss of velocity occurs at every sudden change of direction. A single obstacle may give many shocks and therefore cause several successive losses. Almost always there are two shocks, one at striking the obstacle and the other at leaving it. If the motion between these is curvilinear, never changing its direction suddenly, these two are the only losses.

52. *The loss of velocity when a vehicle strikes an obstacle is* $Vh \div R$.

The car or wagon is here supposed to have two wheels and both to strike the obstacle. The centres of the wheels, as at C (fig. 5) cease to move in the line CG, and begin to move in CH, which is perpendicular to CE, since for a moment E is the centre of motion about which C revolves. The centre of gravity is all the while directly above the line joining the centres of two wheels, and therefore changes its direction exactly as the centres of the wheels change theirs.

Now the former velocity is to the new velocity as CG:CH or as CE:CD or as CB:CD. Hence the former velocity is to the loss of velocity as CB:CB–CD or as CB:BD, or V: loss of velocity::R:h, or loss of velocity is$=$V$h \div$R.

54. *The loss of velocity increases as the velocity of the vehicle and the height of the obstacle directly, and as the radius of the wheel inversely.*

This follows from the formula, the loss equals V$h \div$R. It is greater as the car moves more rapidly, or as it meets a higher obstacle, or as the radius of the wheel is decreased.

55. *If only one wheel strike the obstacle, the loss is only* $\frac{1}{2} Vh \div R$.

For the centre of gravity is between the two wheels, and is now only raised half as much as when both strike. The change of direction, and therefore the loss is also halved.

56. *If the vehicle have four wheels and only one strike the obstacle, the loss is only* $\frac{1}{4} Vh \div R$.

For the centre of gravity is halfway between the two axles, and is raised only half as much as the middle of the axle, that is half as much as in the preceding article.

57. *When the wheels pass over the obstacle and strike the ground again, the loss is usually the same as at meeting the obstacle.*

For the shock and change of direction are usually the same in both cases. On a railway, the loss at the joints of the rails is not doubled, there being but one shock; but it is doubled when a pebble or other obstruction is on the rails.

58. *The force lost is found by multiplying the load into the loss of velocity.*

Because force, being a momentum, is the product of a weight into velocity.

59. *On a railway, as the weight and velocity are large and the joints of the rails numerous, their evenness is of great importance.*

When the iron is first laid down, the two contiguous rails are easily placed in one plane; but from the unequal settling of the sills, and the lateral pressure of the flanges on the wheels, the end of one rail is raised above the other, or moved outward beyond it. The road then becomes rough and uneven, and the loss from obstacles is large.

60. *The use of good springs is of great importance in lessening this resistance.*

When the car or wagon meets an obstacle, the loss is not from lifting the load over the obstacle. It is from the shock, or from the sudden change of direction. When springs are used the wheels still receive the shock, but the load is raised gradually and the loss is much lessened.

61. *Besides the loss of power, the jars and jolts do harm to the cars and the locomotive, damage the freight, and cause discomfort to the passengers.*

The wear and tear of locomotives is a larger item of expense than the cost of fuel, and the jars at the joints are the cause of a great part of this outlay. The difference in comfort between a smooth and well-laid road and one with the rails displaced is immense, but cannot be expressed by numbers.

62. *The resistance of the air on common roads is insensible.*

This is true because of the low velocity and the small front surface presented by a common vehicle.

63. *On a railway the flange friction caused by a high side wind is considerable.*

The flange being so far from the centre of motion, and being rough and unoiled, presents a large resistance when it rubs against the rail.

64. *The head resistance caused by the striking of a train against the air increases as the surface and as the square of the velocity.*

This is shown in Nat. Philosophy to be true of all bodies moving through fluids of any kind.

65. *When the train is moving twenty miles an hour, the head resistance is equal to one pound on each foot of the front surface.*

Instead of regarding the cars as striking the air, we may suppose them at rest, and the air rushing against them with the velocity of the train. To estimate this effect, suppose the air to be contained in a tall close vessel, having an opening of one foot square towards the car, and rushing out of this opening against the car on account of the downward pressure of the air in the close vessel. The velocity with which it will issue, will depend upon the height of the column of air pressing downwards in the tube. And by the laws of spouting fluids, the velocity would be the same as a heavy body would acquire in falling through the height of the vessel. And thus knowing the height of the vessel we learn the velocity of the air; and conversely, if we know the velocity, we learn the height of the column. Thus, suppose the velocity to be 20 miles per hour, or 28⅗ feet per second, the space through which a body must fall to acquire this velocity, is 12.8 feet per second, since $S=\frac{V^2}{4m}$. Hence a column of air 12.8 high may be regarded as pressing against the car at a velocity of 28⅗ feet per second, or 30 miles per hour. The weight of this is nearly one pound, since at 60 degrees air is 815 times lighter than water, and 12.8 feet of water weigh 800 pounds.

A similar result may be obtained from Hutton's experiments on cannon balls. At a velocity of 900 feet per second, the resistance of the air on a ball 2.78 inches in diameter was found to be 35.4 pounds. Now the front is $2.78^2 \times .7854$ or 6 inches. Hence the resistance for a square foot is 24 ×35.4 lbs.=849.6 lbs. For a velocity of $28\frac{2}{3}$ feet per second, the resistance is $849.6 \times 28\frac{2}{3}^2 \div 900^2$ or .93lbs.

This result is a little less than the former, because the rounded form of the ball somewhat lessens the resistance. In both cases however, the result is very near one pound.

66. *The head resistance of a railway train is sensible at common velocities, and very great at high velocities.*

A car has seldom less than 60 feet front surface, the resistance then at 20 miles per hour is 60 lbs. or the same as if a weight of 60 lbs. was suspended by a rope passing over a pulley, and fastened behind the car. This 60 lbs. would be equivalent to 60 lbs.×240=14400 lbs. placed upon the wheels, since one pound hung behind the car is equal to 240 on the wheels on a level way. At 10 miles per hour this additional load is 3600 lbs. At 100 miles it is 360000 lbs. or 180 tons. At this high velocity no common locomotive could overcome the resistance of the air.

LECTURE V.

RESISTANCE OF WATER.

67. *In water, as in air, the resistance is very nearly as the surface, and as the square of the velocity.*

This is true of all fluids, but in the case of water it has been established by many experiments. The most satisfactory of these were made by Col. Beaufoy of England, and conducted as follows: A rope was attached to a body in water, and passed horizontally under a pulley, and then vertically over a very high one, and then attached to a weight. As this weight descended, it first moved the body in the water slowly, and then more rapidly, until the increased resistance of the water balanced the moving force of the weight and the motion became uniform. When this was attained, the weight measured the resistance of the water at the uniform velocity.

Thus to select two of his experiments, a weight of 12 lbs. and then of 48, was attached to the rope and gave the following velocities to a boat in each successive second:

	3.64	4.94	6.68	7.20	7.24	7.36	7.31	7.33
and	5.71	8.78	12.32	13.59	14.02	14.25	14.24	14.31.

The last three, when the motion was nearly uniform, show that a quadruple weight was necessary to give double the velocity, or that the weight increased as the square of the velocity. And in like manner it was shown that this increased as the surface.

68. *The force necessary to overcome the resistance, is as the cube of the velocity.*

For to give double the velocity, the momentum of the moving weight was increased eight times, viz: 12 lbs. with a velocity of 7 feet in the first case, was increased to 48 lbs. with a velocity of 14 feet per second. That is, it is increased as the cube of the velocity. And so for the other velocities.

69. *The work done in transporting a body a given distance, increases as the square of the velocity.*

For the force at each instant increases as the cube of the velocity, and the time during which that force is exerted decreases as the velocity; therefore the work done or FT varies as $V^3 \div V$ or as V^2.

With double the velocity the quadruple weight went twice as fast, but it moved only for half the time to transport the body a given distance. In the first experiment the 12 lbs. moving 21 feet in three seconds transported the body

21 feet. In the second, 48 lbs. moving 42 feet in three seconds transported the body 42 feet. Thus eight times the force doubled the work done, or four times the force did the same work, when the velocity was doubled.

70 *The resistance of a body moving through the water is three-fold, the head resistance, the plus and minus pressure, and the friction of the whole surface.*

The first is caused by striking against the particles of water; the second by a greater pressure from the water in front than at the stern, when the boat is in motion; and the third by the adhesion of the water to the body.

71. *When the relocity is one mile per hour, the head resis tance is about $2\frac{1}{8}$ lbs. for each square foot, if the bow is a plane perpendicular to the keel.*

To determine this resistance, suppose the boat at rest and the water moving against it. The water may be supposed to be confined in a tall close vessel, having an opening towards the boat and rushing against it on account of the downward pressure of the water in the close vessel. The height of this water is found by means of the formula $S=\frac{V^2}{4m}$. For one mile per hour, or $1\frac{7}{15}$ feet per second, $S=\frac{1}{30}$ of a foot, and $\frac{1}{30}$ of a foot of water weighs $2\frac{1}{12}$ lbs. or nearly $2\frac{1}{8}$. For a velocity of two miles, this would give $8\frac{1}{2}$ lbs; for three miles it would be $19\frac{1}{8}$ lbs; for four miles it would be 34lbs.

Beaufoy's experiments gave for these four velocities 2.19, 8.6, 19.2, and 34 lbs.

72. *If the bow be sharpened, the head resistance decreases nearly as the sine of the angle which the side of the vessel makes with the keel of the boat.*

This follows from the decomposition of forces. With a bow of 15^0 and a velocity of five miles an hour, this would give $53\frac{1}{8}\times$ sin. 15^0 or 13.74 lbs. For a bow of 10^0 it gives 9.20 lbs.

Beaufoy's experiments gave for these angles at this velocity 13.26, and 9.21 lbs.

73. *For sharp well shaped boats the head resistance is about $\frac{1}{3}$ of a lb; for blunt boats, it is about $\frac{1}{2}$ of a lb; when the velocity is one mile per hour.*

The first corresponds to a sharpness of 9 or 10^0, the second to 14 or 15^0. The first is the shape of ships and steam-boats, the second of canal boats.

74. *The plus and minus pressure of boats is about $\frac{1}{5}$ of the head resistance.*

This is caused by the piling up of the water in front, and the vacuum formed behind the boat.

In narrow canals this resistance is still greater, because the water in front cannot readily get round the sides of the boat.

75. *The friction is about 1 lb. for every 150 feet of surface in contact with the water, when the velocity is one mile per hour.*

This is about the result of Beaufoy's experiments.

76. *The resistance on a common canal boat at $2\frac{1}{2}$ miles per hour, is about $\frac{1}{720}$ of the load.*

In an experiment of Mr. Bevan on the Grand Junction Canal, a weight of 77 lbs. produced a velocity of $2\frac{1}{2}$ miles per hour, when the load was 21 tons, and the weight of the boat 9 tons. Here the resistance was $77 \div 30 \times 2240$ or $\frac{1}{853}$.— The width of the Canal where this experiment was made was 142 feet; and in a narrow canal 40 or 50 feet wide, according to the experiments of Stephenson, the resistance was about $\frac{1}{5}$ more, which would give $\frac{1}{711}$.

If we suppose a boat to be 70 feet long, 12 feet wide, and sunk 2 feet in the water by its load, the weight of the water displaced, that is, the weight of the boat and its load will be $70 \times 12 \times 2 \times 62\frac{1}{2}$, or 105000 lbs.

The head resistance for a velocity of $2\frac{1}{2}$ miles per hour will be $12 \times 2 \times \frac{1}{2} \times 2\frac{1}{2}^2$ or 75 lbs. The plus and minus pressure will be $\frac{1}{5}$ of 75 lbs. or 15 lbs. The friction will be $16 \times 70 \times 2\frac{1}{2}^2 \div 150$ or $46\frac{2}{3}$ lbs. Hence the total resistance is $75 + 15 + 46\frac{2}{3}$, or $136\frac{2}{3}$ lbs. and this is the $\frac{1}{769}$ part of 105000 lbs. the whole load; so that the total resistance is nearly $\frac{1}{270}$ of the load.

77. *On a canal the locks should be long, the canal wide and deep.*

When the locks are long, the boats may be made long,

and thus the head resistance for the same load is lessened. When the canal is wide, the plus and minus pressure is decreased. When the canal is deep, the friction will not increase as fast as the load, since if the load is doubled and the boat thus sunk twice as deep in the water, the surface in contact is but little increased.

78. *High velocities in water can only be obtained by a large expenditure of force.*

At $2\frac{1}{2}$ miles per hour the resistance is $\frac{1}{720}$ of the load, or one third of the amount on a rail-road. At 5 miles per hour it is $\frac{4}{720}$ of the load, or one third more than it is on the rail-road. At 10 miles an hour it is $\frac{16}{720}$ of the load, or more than five times as much as on a rail-road. At 20 miles per hour it is $\frac{64}{720}$ of the load, or nearly twice as much as on a common hard road.

LECTURE VI.

POWERS.

79. *The unit by which the Engineer measures his several powers, is a horse-power, which is the momentum of 150 lbs. raised vertically at the rate of $2\frac{1}{2}$ miles per hour.*

This is rather above the average power of a horse, but if a strong horse be attached to a rope passing horizontally over a pulley, to which 150 lbs. is suspended, as in a well, he will be able to move at the rate of $2\frac{1}{2}$ miles per hour, and continue that effort through the whole day. This horse-power of the Engineer is, however a fixed, invariable quantity, and not dependant upon the power of a horse having average or superior strength.

89. *Other expressions for a horse-power are 375 lbs. raised at the rate of one mile per hour, 33000 lbs. raised at the rate of one foot per minute, and 528 cuibc feet of water raised one foot high per minute.*

For the momentum of all of these weights is the same; thus $150\times 2\frac{1}{2}=375\times 1$ & $375\times 5280\div 60=33000\times 1$ and $33.000\div 62\frac{1}{2}=528$.

A horse, by acting on a lever, or by a rope passing over a wheel, can raise either of these weights 150, or 375, or 33000 lbs, but the velocity of the larger weights would be so much diminished that their momentum would remain the same.

81. *For the horse-power required to transport a load on a common road or a railroad, find the gravity by the formula* $WHV\div L$, *and the friction which is equal to* $WV\div 20$, *or* $WV\div 240$, *and the sum of friction and gravity divided by 375 will give the number of horse-power.*

Example. If a load of 6000 lbs. be moved at the rate of $2\frac{1}{2}$ miles per hour, on a firm hard road, rising 1 foot in 10, the horse-power required is 6; for the friction is 750 lbs. and gravity is 1500 lbs. and their sum 2250 divided by 375 gives 6.

If the road were level, the horse-power required would be 2.

If the road descended 1 foot in 40, the horse-power required would be 1.

If the velocity had been 5 miles per hour in each of these cases, the horse-power would be 12, 4, and 2.

On a railway rising 44 feet in a mile, if a gross load of 120 tons, of 2000 lbs. each, move at the rate of 10 miles per hour, the horse-power required would be 80, for the friction is 10000 lbs, and gravity is 20000 and their sum divided by 375 will give 80.

If the road rise 22 feet in a mile the horse-power would be $53\frac{1}{3}$.

If the road were level the horse-power would be $26\frac{2}{3}$.

82. *On a canal the resistance at $2\frac{1}{2}$ miles per hour is $W\div 720$ and this divided by 150 will give the horse-power.*

If a load of 54 tons were drawn at $2\frac{1}{2}$ miles per hour, the horse-power required would be 1.

83. *For the horse-power on a canal at any velocity, find the resistance at that velocity and divide it by the horse-power at that velocity.*

EXAMPLE. If a load of 36 tons be drawn at a velocity of 6 miles per hour, the horse-power required would be about 9. For the resistance at $2\frac{1}{2}$ miles per hour, being W ÷720, it would be, at 1 mile per hour, $W \div 720 \times 2\frac{1}{2}^2$, or W÷ 4500; and for six miles per hour it would be 36 W÷ 4500 or W÷ 125. And a horse-power at 1 mile per hour being 375 lbs, it would be $62\frac{1}{2}$ lbs. at 6 miles per hour. Now in this example, W being 36× 2000 lbs. the resistance, W÷125, is 576, and $576 \div 62\frac{1}{2}$ gives about 9.

If the velocity is 10 miles per hour the resistance would be W÷ 45, and a horse-power would be $37\frac{1}{2}$, and the number of horse-power required to move the load at this velocity would be $42\frac{2}{3}$.

The horse-power required to draw 120 tons on a level hard common road, and on a common road rising one foot in 20, and on a level rail-road, and on a rail-road rising 22 feet in a mile, and on a canal, at velocities of $2\frac{1}{2}$, 4, and 6 miles per hour would be, for the first road 80, 128, and 192; for the second, they would be 160, 256 and 384; and for the third they would be $6\frac{2}{3}$, $10\frac{2}{3}$, and 16; for the fourth they would be $13\frac{1}{3}$ $21\frac{1}{3}$, and 32: for the fifth they would be $2\frac{2}{9}$, about 9.1, and about 31.

84. *For the horse-power of a steam engine, multiply together the number of inches in the piston, the number of pounds pressing on each inch, and the number of feet the piston moves through in a minute, and divide the product by* 33000.

For the piston may be regarded as a weight equal to the number of pounds pressing on its whole surface, and the momentum of this weight, is the power of the engine.

If the steam be cut off before the piston makes its full stroke, the average pressure for the whole stroke must be taken.

EXAMPLE. If a piston 10 inches in diameter, with a pressure on it of 50 lbs. to the square inch, make 110 double strokes 2 feet long, per minute, its horse-power would be 52.

For the area of the piston is 78 inches, the weight in motion is 50×78, or 3900; the velocity is 110×4, or 440 feet per minute; the momentum is 3900×440, and the horse-power is $3900\times 440\div 33000$, or 52.

85. *To find the force of a water-fall, multiply the weight of the water passing in a minute, by the number of feet in the fall, and divide by* 33000.

EXAMPLE. If a stream 20 feet wide and 1 foot deep, should move at the rate of 3 feet per second, and have a fall of 11 feet, it would have 75 horse-power.

For the weight of water passing over in a minute is $20\times 3\times 60\times 62\frac{1}{2}$, or 225000. And this $\times\ 11\div 33000$ gives 75.

86. *The velocity of the water issuing from the opening in a flume, may be found by the formula,* $V^2=4mS$ or $V=8\surd S$.

EXAMPLE. Suppose a flume to have an opening 16 feet wide, 3 inches deep, and the middle of the opening to be 27 inches below the head of the water, and the fall to be 11 feet, the horse-power would be 60.

For $S=27$ inches, or $2\frac{1}{4}$ feet, and $V=8$ times the square root of $2\frac{1}{4}$, or 12 feet; the area of the opening is $16\times\frac{1}{4}$ or 4 feet; the quantity of water falling in a minute is $4\times 12\times 60$ or 2880 feet; its weight is $2880\times 62\frac{1}{2}$ or 180000 lbs; and $180000\times 11\div 33000=60$ horse-power.

The stream passing through the opening is smaller than the opening itself, and a deduction of one-third should be made from the amount of water delivered, for this cause.

87. *The horse-power required for a saw-mill cutting* 1000 *feet of plank per day, is* 3; *for a grist mill running one pair of stones, is* 5; *for a cotton mill, one for every two hundred spindles, and one for every twelve looms.*

These are the net amounts, after deduction is made for the loss of power on the water wheels, and the friction of the machinery.

LECTURE VII.

THE POWER OF THE HORSE.

88. *The power of a horse of average strength, is 125 lbs. raised vertically at the rate of 2½ miles per hour, and continued for eight hours in the day.*

Watt's estimate was 150 lbs.; Desagulier's 200 lbs.; but these were early estimates, and have since been found too high. A set of trials published in "Wood's Treatise on Railroads" gives an average as low as 100 lbs. But in these the horse drew at times from 250 to 320 lbs. and when such excessive exertion is required, the horse cannot do as much work as if the changes were more moderate. Smeaton's estimate was also 100 lbs.; Tredgold and Fraley put it at 125 lbs.

The common gross load for a horse on a canal is 40 tons, at 2½ miles per hour, which would give 111 lbs. since resistance is $\frac{1}{720}$.

In the cities where the streets are level and paved, the usual load of a dray horse is 3000 lbs. and this would give 150 lbs. as the vertical load, but the best horses are used for this purpose. On good roads where the maximum rise is limited by law to 1 in 20, the usual load is 1700 lbs. and this would give 85 lbs. on the level, and 170 lbs. on the ascents, or an average of 127½ lbs. On the mountain roads where the greatest rise is limited by law to 1 in 12, the usual load is 1200 lbs. and this would give 60 lbs. on the level, and 160 on the ascents, or an average of 110 lbs. On our hilly roads the rise is often 1 in 8 and the load 1000 lbs.; this would give 50 lbs. on the level, and 175 on the ascents, or an average of 112½.

In all these cases the average is a little less than 125, but something must be allowed for obstacles, so that **125** lbs. may be regarded as the power exerted by a horse of average strength.

89. *The day's work of a horse is* 5000 *lbs. raised vertically through one mile.*

For the 125 lbs. is moved at the rate of $2\frac{1}{2}$ miles per hour, and the horse continues his work 8 hours. And $125\times2\frac{1}{2}\times 8=5000$.

90. *The force required to move the horse's body, is about* 125 *lbs. multiplied by the velocity.*

For it is found by experience that he can raise 125 lbs. and move his body 20 miles in a day; and without any load, that he can move his body 40 miles per day; in both cases traveling 8 hours per day. Hence if B represent the weight raised vertically which is equivalent to moving his body forward, we have $(125+B)\ 20=40B$. Hence $B=125$ lbs.

In the first case the momentum is $(125+B)\ 2\frac{1}{2}$ or $250\times 2\frac{1}{2}$ or 625; in the second case the momentum is 5B or 125×5 or 625.

91. *When the momentum required of the horse is less than* 625 *lbs. he can work longer than eight hours, so that his whole day's work shall equal* 5000 *lbs. raised* 1 *mile.*

Thus if his load is only 25 lbs. raised vertically, and he travels 4 miles per hour, the momentum exerted is $(25+B)\ 4$, or 600 lbs.; and the hours he can work are $5000\div 600$ or $8\frac{1}{3}$; and the distance he can travel is $8\frac{1}{3}\times 4$ or $33\frac{1}{3}$ miles. This is the proper load when a horse travels with a light buggy over a good level or undulating road, and this is the distance he can travel with such a load day after day without resting.

92. *When the momentum required of the horse exceeds* 625 *lbs. the work done per day is decreased in proportion to the excess.*

Thus if his load is 60 lbs. raised vertically, and he travels 5 miles per hour, the momentum is $(60+125)\ 5$ or 925 lbs. And 925: 625::5000: 3379 which is the work he can do in a day. This 3379 divided by 925 gives 3.6 as the number of hours he can work in the day. And 3.6×5 or 18 miles is the distance he can travel in a day. This is about the load and velocity for stage horses on good roads; but it is common to have a heavier load and travel 20 miles per day; but this always results in injury to the horses.

The greatest force a horse can exert without injury, is about double this momentum, or 1250 lbs. Thus if, unloaded he travels more than ten miles per hour, his momentum would be above 1250 lbs.; or if with a load equal to 90 lbs. raised vertically he travel 6 miles per hour; or if with a load equal to 300 lbs. raised vertically he travel 3 miles per hour; in all these cases his exertion will be excessive and injurious.

93. *The cost of transportation on common roads, when horses are advantageously employed, is $12 per ton.*

Thus if five horses should carry a net load of 4000 lbs. 100 miles, and have the same back load, the time consumed would be ten days in traveling, and two in loading and unloading, and this load at $12 per ton, would pay $4.00 per day for the team.

94. *If only two horses are used, or if there be no back load, the cost of transportation is about $20 per ton, for 100 miles, or one cent for 100 lbs. per mile.*

Thus if five horses should carry a net load of 4000 lbs. 60 miles, and return unloaded, the time employed would be 3 days going, two returning, and one loading, or 6 days in all; and the load at 60 cts. per hundred, would amount to $24; which would give $4 per day.

95. *On a rail-road where the maximum rise is 36 feet per mile, the cost of transportation by horses would be about $1.75 per ton, per 100 miles.*

For a gross load of 16 tons would give for friction 16 X 2000÷240 or 133 lbs. and for gravity on the ascents 32000 X 36÷5280 or 218 lbs.; so that the load on the level is 133 lbs. and on the ascents 133+218 or 351 lbs. and the average is 242, which would be about the load for two horses. Of these 16 tons, the net load would be about 10 tons. To carry this load 100 miles would require 5 days for traveling, and 2 for loading and unloading. And 10 tons at

$1.75 for 7 days would give $2.50 per day, which would be a fair compensation.

96. *On a canal the cost of transportation is about* 50 *cts. per* 100 *miles, if a load can be had in both directions.*

The common net load for two horses on a canal is about 80 tons of 2000 lbs. each. The boat will increase this load to 90 tons, or 180000 lbs. The resistance to this load at 2½ miles per hour, 180000÷ 720, or 250 lbs. which is the power of two horses. Now $5 per day would be about the proper pay for two horses, for two men and a boy, and for the wear and tear of the boat. This for 7 days employed in the trip would make $35; and $5 for extra labor of loading and unloading would make $40; and $40÷80 would be 50 cts. per ton.

LECTURE VIII.

THE STEAM ENGINE.

97. *The first application of steam to useful purposes was by Savery, in the year* 1700.

Before the Christian era Hero proposed the use of steam to produce motion. In the 17th century several inventors explained how steam might be employed for this effect. But Savery in England, first constructed an engine in which steam was actually applied to useful purposes. In this the steam was used to raise water from the mines. As it acted immediately on the water and required boilers of great strength, it was of but slight utility.

98. *A piston was first used by Newcomen and Savery, in* 1712.

This saved the immense loss of steam which was occasioned by its coming in contact with the water, and enabled the inventors, by having the steam-piston large and the pump-piston small, to raise water to any height, with steam of moderate strength. Their engine was called the Atmospheric engine, because the motive power was the Atmosphere, steam being used only to produce a vacuum. This was extensively used in the English mines to raise water, and where fuel was cheap, it was of great advantage.

99. *The real inventor of the Steam Engine was James Watt.*

By driving the piston by the steam itself, by encasing the cylinder so as to keep it all the while hot, by cutting off the steam before it had driven the piston its full stroke, and by various minor improvements he saved five-sixths of the steam used in Newcomen's engines, and made his engine applicable to other purposes besides the raising of water. Watt's first engine was constructed in 1776.

100. *The steamboat was first successfully introduced by Fulton, on the Hudson river, in* 1807.

Before this time boats had been driven by steam at four or five miles per hour, both on the Delaware, and on the Clyde; but at this velocity a steamboat could not be worked profitably. Fulton obtained a velocity of seven miles per hour, and from that time to this they have never ceased to run on the Hudson. Not until 1812 were they introduced into Great Britian; and not into France, until 1816.

101. *The first locomotive was constructed by Trevithick and Vivian, in* 1804.

The principle of this engine was correct, but it was not successfully introduced until 1830. In that year the Liverpool and Manchester railroad was completed, and an engine was tried at the opening of the road, which carried three times its weight, and moved at the rate of fifteen miles per hour. The improvements since this time have been very great, so that it can now draw 20, and even 30 times its own weight, and move with a velocity of 40 or 50 miles per hour; and for express trains 70 or 80 have been attained.

102. *A locomotive is a steam engine with two cylinders*

whose pistons act upon the radii of the driving wheels, or on a crank which is a part of the axle of these wheels.

If the driving wheels rested on a perfectly smooth surface, the turning of these wheels would not move the locomotive forward. If it rested on such a surface as ice, it would also revolve without moving forward, if the resistance at the rim were less than the other resistance that must be overcome when the train moves forward. And universally, the adhesion at the circumference must exceed the friction at the axles, the gravity of the train, the resistance of the air, and all other forces which oppose the motion of the cars, or else the train will remain stationary.

103. *The greatest load a locomotive can draw, on a level rail-road, is about* 40 *times the weight resting on the driving wheels.*

If a locomotive had its wheels wedged to the axle so that they could not revolve, it could be dragged forward by a weight attached to a rope passing over a pulley, if the weight was $\frac{1}{6}$ of the weight of the locomotive. This has been proved by the experiments of Tredgold, and corresponds with the amount of friction of iron rubbing on iron. Hence if the train stand still, the adhesion at the rim of the driving wheels is $\frac{1}{6}$ of the weight resting on them. If the train move forward the axle friction is $\frac{1}{240}$ of the weight of the train. Whichever of these two is the least will be overcome. Let D be the weight resting on the driving wheels, and W the weight of the train; then if $\frac{D}{6}$ is greater than $\frac{W}{240}$ the train will move; that is, W must be less than 40 D. This weight of the train includes the weight of the engine, and is the gross load moved forwards.

104. *The maximum net load on a level, is usually about* 14 *times the weight of the locomotive.*

The driving wheels may be made to support $\frac{3}{4}$ of the weight of the locomotive. The adhesion is therefore $\frac{1}{6} \times \frac{3}{4}$E, if E represent the weight of the locomotive. The load in the cars usually about equals the weight of the cars themselves. Then if N is the net load, $\frac{1}{240}$ (2N+E) is the friction. And if the adhesion and friction are the same, we have $\frac{1}{6} \times \frac{3}{4}E = \frac{1}{240}(2N+E)$ or $30E = 2N+E$, or $N = 14\frac{1}{2}E$. From this must be deducted the weight of the tender, which will bring down the net load nearly to 14E.

105. *The maximum load is still less on an inclined plane and at high velocities, on account of the resistance of gravity and the air.*

If these several resistances be calculated and compared with the adhesion, we may determine which is the greatest, and therefore whether the train will move forward, or the driving wheels revolve.

EXAMPLE. Can a gross load of 120 tons, be drawn up an inclined plane rising 36 feet in a mile at a velocity of 10 miles per hour, by a locomotive of 12 tons and front surface 60 feet, the tender weighing 6 tons. Here friction is $\frac{W}{240}$ or 1150 lbs.; gravity is $36W \div 5280$, or 1881 lbs.; resistance of the air is $60 \times 10^2 \div 20^2$, or 15 lbs.; total resistance 3046 lbs. The adhesion is $\frac{1}{6}.\frac{3}{4}.12.2000$, or 3000 lbs. so that the load would not advance, since the adhesion is less than the other resistance.

106. *The adhesion may be increased by gearing several wheels together, or by making the locomotive heavier.*

The gearing of the wheels together is rendered difficult on account of the train moving in a curve, where the distance between the wheels is less on the inside and greater on the outside than it is when on the straight part of the road. This causes a slipping of the wheels which occasions much resistance. When however the locomotive is heavier than 14 or 15 tons, it is common to gear together two driving wheels on each side very near each other. As they are very near, the distance between the centres of the two wheels is but slightly changed, and the slipping is therefore small. The advantage of distributing the heavy weight resting on the driving wheels, among four instead of two wheels, is very considerable; since the injury to the road-bed by these heavily loaded wheels moving at high velocities is very great.

107. *Two cylinders are used, to give greater uniformity to the motion of the train.*

The two cranks on the axle being placed at right angles to each other, when the piston-rod of one cylinder is acting at right angles to its crank, and producing its greatest effect, the other piston-rod is in a line with its crank and producing no effect at all. For other positions of the crank, the two rods produce effects less than their maximum, so that the sum of both is nearly constant.

108. *The high-pressure Engine is always used for the Locomotive.*

Because the cold water necessary for condensing the steam in the low-pressure engine could not be supplied or carried conveniently.

109. *The draft is obtained by the escape of the waste steam into the chimney.*

This draft is very important, and the usual mode of obtaining it, in other steam engines by a high chimney, is not convenient on a locomotive. The waste steam escaping with great rapidity up the chimney carries with it the air around it, and produces a vacuum which can only be filled by air passing through the fire. The draught is thus greater as the jets of steam become more frequent, that is as the locomotive moves more rapidly. Thus the greater the velocity of the engine, the greater will be the draft, the more briskly will the fire burn, and the more rapidly will the steam be generated.

110. *The tubular boiler is the only one suited for the locomotive.*

As the weight of the locomotive is part of the load that must be carried forward, it is desirable to have it light and compact, so that the net load may be as great as possible.—The fire-box is therefore surrounded on all sides with water, and the flame and hot air and smoke are carried horizontally through a large number of small copper tubes about two inches in diameter, so as to present a large heating surface to the water, and thus generate the steam rapidly.

111. *The best kind of fuel is rich pine, or any wood that will produce much flame.*

The fire-box being not larger than four feet in every direction, its sides and top will contain 64 square feet. The copper tubes in the boiler being about 8 feet long, and two inches in diameter, 100 of them will have 400 square feet of surface. Thus the surface on which the flame acts is six times larger than that on which the fire acts; and it is therefore important that the fuel should produce much flame.

Coal is used where wood is costly, but the bituminous suits better than the anthracite.

LECTURE IX.

THE STEAM ENGINE CONTINUED.

112. *The velocity of the locomotive depends on the evaporating power of the engine.*

When the locomotive is first started, if the effective pressure on the piston is 60 lbs. per inch, and is sufficient to make the locomotive move faster and faster, its velocity would be increased indefinitely, if the pressure remained the same.—For the motive power is the number of pounds pressing on the piston multiplied by its velocity, and the resistance of the train depends on its weight multiplied by its velocity; and as the two velocities both increase at the same rate, if the first product is greater at first, it will continue greater always, and thus increase without limit the velocity of the train.

But as the train moves faster more cylinders full of steam are wanted; and after a short time more steam is consumed than the boiler can generate at this great strength. The pressure then upon the piston becomes less until the motive power just equals the resistance, and the train moves uniformly.

Thus suppose the piston to have a stroke of 2 feet, and the driving wheels a diameter of 5¼ feet, the velocity of the train will then be $4\frac{1}{8}$ times the velocity of the piston. If the diameter of the piston be 12 inches its area will be about 113 inches, and the whole pressure on it about 60×113. If the weight of the train be 120 tons and the road level, the resistance will be $120 \times 2000 \div 240$ or 1000 lbs. And the moving force which is $60 \times 113 \times 1$ is greater than the resistance, which is $1000 \times 4\frac{1}{8}$. Hence, if the road continued level, and the resistance of the air be not considered, the velocity would increase until the pressure on the piston would be reduced to 40 lbs; for then the motive force 40×113 would about equal $1000 \times 4\frac{1}{8}$. The train would now move uniformly, the boiler being just able to produce as much steam as is wanted at a pressure of 40 lbs.

113. *The volume of steam a boiler can produce depends on the strength of steam that is required.*

If a boiler can evaporate one cubic foot of water at the temperature of 212° at which its pressure is about 15 lbs., the same amount of water can be evaporated by the same fire at a pressure of 30 lbs.; but the bulk of the steam will only be half as large as before. So for other pressures, the volume is, very nearly, inversely as the pressure.

114. *The amount of steam generated in a good locomotive when the fire is burning briskly is about 500 cubic feet per hour at a pressure of 15 lbs. for every square foot in the tubes of the boiler, and three times as much for every square foot in the fire-box.*

This is the result of experiments made by Pambour on the Liverpool & Manchester Road.

For the engine mentioned above in article 111, where the fire-box contained 64 feet, and the tubes 400 feet, the steam generated in an hour at a pressure of 15 lbs., would be $400 \times 500 + 500 \times 64 \times 3$ or 296000 feet.

115. *The velocity at which a given load can be drawn by a given engine will be obtained, by finding the pressure that must be exerted on the piston to move the given load, and then finding how many cylinders full of steam the boiler can generate at that pressure.*

Example Suppose a locomotive of 12 tons, generate

steam as in the last article (114), and has cylinders 12 feet in diameter with 2 feet stroke, and driving wheels $5\frac{1}{4}$ feet in diameter, what velocity can it attain, on a railroad rising 36 feet in a mile, with a gross load of 120 tons, and a tender of 6 tons.

Here the mass moved is 138×2000 or 276000 lbs.; the friction is $276000 \div 240$ or 1150 lbs.; the gravity is $276000 \times 36 \div 5280$ or 1881 lbs. The sum of these two resistances is 3031. For every double stroke of the piston the driving wheels make one revolution; that is, while the piston moves 4 feet, the train moves $16\frac{1}{2}$. Hence, the pressure on the piston must exceed the resistance in the ratio of $16\frac{1}{2}$ to 4, so that the moving force should balance the resistance. Hence, the pressure on the pistons is $3031 \times 16\frac{1}{2} \div 4$ or 12503 lbs. But the two pistons have an area of $12^2 \times .7854 \times 2$ or 226 inches. Hence, the effective pressure of the steam on each square inch must be $12503 \div 226$ or 55 lbs. The real pressure must be 15 lbs. more than this, because of the resistance of the atmosphere on the other side of the piston; and 4 or 5 more, because of the backward pressure of the escape steam. The total pressure of the steam must be therefore $55+15+5$ or 75 lbs.

Now as the boiler can generate in an hour 296000 feet of steam at 15 lbs. pressure, the amount at 75 lbs. pressure will be $296000 \div 5$ or 59200 feet. The two cylinders contain $2 \times 2 \times 1^2 \times .7854$ or 3.14 solid feet. Hence, $59200 \div 3.14$ or 18840 will express the number of times both cylinders will be filled in an hour. The double strokes will be $18840 \div 2$ or 9420. And finally the velocity of the train will be $9420 \times 16\frac{1}{2} \div 5280$ or $29\frac{1}{2}$ miles per hour.

In this calculation no allowance is made for the resistance of the air, so that the real velocity will be less than $29\frac{1}{2}$ miles. If it be taken at $28\frac{1}{2}$, the resistance on 60 square feet front will be $60 \times 28\frac{1}{2}^2 \div 20^2$ or 122 lbs. If this be added to the resistance of friction and gravity, and the calculation repeated, the real velocity will be more accurately obtained. The resistance of the train will be 3153 lbs. The pressure on the piston, 13007 lbs. The effective pressure per inch, $57\frac{1}{2}$ lbs. The steam generated at the required pressure in one hour,

57290 feet. The number of double strokes 8118. And the velocity $28\frac{1}{2}$ miles per hour.

116. *It is best to use steam of strong pressure, that is of four or five atmospheres.*

For although it takes twice as much fuel to generate the same volume of steam at 80 lbs. pressure as at 40, yet since the steam is thrown away still retaining a force of 19 or 20 lbs. the effective pressure of the first is 80—20 or 60 lbs. and of the second 40—20 or 20 lbs.; that is, in this case the effect is trebled while the fuel is only doubled.

117. *The greatest useful effect is produced at low velocities.*

This is true for two reasons; because at low velocities the fire is able to generate steam of strong pressure, and therefore according to the last article to produce the greatest effect. And again, because although, with half the velocity and double the effective pressure, the gross work done would remain the same, yet the net load, after the tender and engine are deducted, would decrease faster than the velocity would increase; and thus the work done would diminish. Thus, if a given evaporating power would move a gross load of 60 tons at 20 miles per hour, and the same amount of steam would move 120 tons at 10 miles per hour, the net load in the two cases would be 42 and 102 tons, if the engine and tender together weighed 18 tons. But 102 tons at 10 miles per hour is a greater useful effect than 42 tons at 20 miles per hour.

118. *When a Railroad has a single ascent of 80 or 90 feet in a mile, the usual maximum grades on the road being 40 or 50 feet, an additional Locomotive is sometimes used to draw the train up this ascent, but more commonly a stationary steam engine is employed.*

On a level the greatest load a locomotive can draw is 40 times the weight resting on the driving wheels; the adhesion being $\frac{1}{6}$ of this weight, and the resistance of the train being $\frac{1}{240}$ of the load. On an inclined plane rising 22 feet in a mile, gravity is $22 \div 5280$ or $\frac{1}{240}$. So that the whole resistance is now doubled, and the maximum load is only . 20

times the weight resting on the driving wheels. If the plane rises 44 feet in a mile, gravity is twice as much as the friction, and both are $_{240}$; so that the load is $13\frac{1}{3}$ times the weight on the driving wheels. If the plane rises 88 feet in a mile, gravity is 4 times the friction, and the total resistance is $\frac{5}{240}$; and the maximum load is only 8 times the weight resting on the driving wheels.

Now it is better economy to accommodate the load to what can be drawn on the common ascents, and to keep an additional force at the single steep plane, rather than to reduce the load to its amount for the steep plane, and to have only half or quarter of the load suited for the engine on the other parts of the road.

119. *When full work can be found for the steam engine, it is always cheaper than animal power.*

This is true whether the engine is of 5 horse-power, of 20, or 100; whether employed on a saw-mill, a grist mill, or a factory of any kind. But on a rail-road a locomotive is not much cheaper than horses. On the Georgia rail-road the cost of carrying 1 ton 100 miles is about \$1.35, and this is cheaper than it is on most other roads. The cost of horses for the same work would be \$1.75, so that the difference in expense is small.

120. *The greatest advantage of a locomotive is the rapidity and regularity with which it moves, and the large amount of work it can perform on a single road.*

The saving of time is important not only to the passengers, but to the owners of freight. This is especially true when the freight is of a costly kind, such as dry goods, drugs or jewelry. On these, the interest on the money invested in them for the time saved by the locomotive would often pay the whole cost of transportation.

On the Reading rail-road they transport from the mines about 6000 tons of coal per day. Every hour 500 tons must be started from the terminus, and if we allow 10 tons for a load for two horses, it would be necessary to start 50 teams in an hour. As these would be so numerous, and so near each other, an accident to one would delay many others.

The breaking of a trace, or an injury to a horse or to a car, would render it impossible to perform the work; for there would be no time to repair the injury before other teams would overtake them.

Thus the locomotive excels animal power, not so much in its cheapness, as in the amount of its work and the rapidity with which it is done.

LECTURE X.

GRAVITY AND WATER POWER.

121. *Gravity can seldom be used advantageously as a motive power.*

If the merchandise to be transported is equal in both directions, the loss and gain from gravity would balance each other. Thus on a rail-road continually descending, the freight might be carried without steam or animal power in one direction, but the increased force necessary to return would equal the gain in going down. So on a river; the boat descends of itself, but the extra force required to ascend the stream prevents us from gaining any advantage by the descending current.

Even if the freight is all in the downward direction, gravity is but of little benefit. On rivers, if the descent is slight, the boat will move slowly, and the cost of attendance for a given distance will be large. If the current is more rapid, the expense of returning the empty boat, or of building a new one for a second trip will be considerable; and in both these cases it is usually found best to use the steamboat instead of the flat boat or floating box or ark. If the stream is very rapid, the expense of returning the boats and the liability to injuries from the bending of the stream, and from rapids, snags and other obstructions will be very considerable. On long rail-roads, since the descent must be over 22 feet per mile to move the cars by gravity, this motive power can seldom be used. On short roads, if the freight is all in one direction, as from a coal mine to a navigable river, gravity may be used to some advantage. If the road is very short and the descent large, the loaded cars may be used to draw up the empty ones, and then gravity is of decided advantage. It thus appears that this force although furnished by nature without any expense, can almost never be used advantageously as a prime mover.

122. *A water fall is a force furnished by nature, and is the cheapest power that can be employed.*

This is only true where the water is abundant, constant, convenient to the work to be performed, and obtained by a dam of moderate expense. For if the water fail to perform the work, or is dependent upon the seasons, or is out of the way so that the work has to be carried to it, or requires a large outlay for the building of a dam and keeping it in repairs, steam may be cheaper than water power.

123. *The several wheels employed in using water, are the* Overshot, *the* Breast, *the* Undershot, *the* Flutter, *and the* Re-action *wheels.*

The first four are vertical wheels, and the last horizontal. In the overshot, the water acts by its weight; in the flutter and undershot, by its impulse; in the reaction, by its pressure; but in all, the full effect of the water depends on its amount, and the height of the fall. A larger or a smaller portion of this power is, however, always lost.

124. *In using the overshot wheels the loss varies from one-fifth to one-third of the full effect of the water.*

This is occasioned in part by spilling the water out of the buckets, but mainly because the water, when it leaves the wheel, must have at least the velocity of the wheel, and therefore cannot transfer to it its whole momentum.

The spilling of the water should be prevented by an arc or apron fitting close to the rim of the wheel. The momentum retained by the moving water will be lessened by making the wheel revolve very slowly. But this slowness has a limit in practice, since the water must move with sufficient velocity to keep clear of the wheel. According to Smeaton's experiments, in which the fullest confidence is placed, the velocity of the rim should be 3 feet per second.

125. *The water should have a slight head, so as to strike the wheel with at least the velocity of the wheel.*

If it should fall with less velocity, it would at first be a retarding rather than a moving force. If it should fall with a greater velocity, some of the water would rebound and then drive off particles from striking the wheel.

The head need not be more than a foot, for this fall would give a velocity of 8 feet per second, by the formula $V=8\sqrt{S}$, no allowance being made for retardation by friction.

126. *The water should be so directed as to strike the wheel at right angles with the radii.*

Otherwise, some of its momentum would be lost by not being in the direction of the moving body. This should be particularly attended to when the water is made to fall on the wheel on the upper side. For then, unless the water is guided, the direction would not be at all right.

127. *It is best to apply the water on the upper side and below the top of the wheel.*

For if on the upper side, the back water at the bottom will not be so likely to retard the wheel; and by striking below the top, the water is more easily guided in the proper direction.

128. *The buckets should be formed of two parts, one in the direction of the radii and the other at an angle of* 120° *with the first. Fig.* 15.

If the side of the bucket were at right angles with the bottom, all the water could not escape till the bucket reached the lowest part of the wheel. As its escape would require a little time, some would be carried past the lowest point, and then by acting backwards retard the wheel.

With the proper shape, the water would all escape from

6

the buckets, when the wheel was at rest, 30^0 above the lowest point; but when in motion, it would remain longer and only complete its escape when it reached the lowest point of the wheel.

129. *The diameter of the wheel may exceed the fall about one-eighth of its height.*

The water must then be admitted on the upper side, as it cannot run over the high wheel. This eighth of the fall, added to the height of the head above the opening in the flume, will make the water strike the wheel 35 or 40^0 from the top, where it may be easily put on the wheel in the proper direction.

130. *In an undershot wheel, the loss of power is about two-thirds of the full effect of the water.*

In this case the water acts by its impulse and not by its weight. It does not fall into buckets, but strikes against floats which are at right angles to the rim of the wheel. For these reasons the water and the wheel must both move with considerable velocity. And hence the water leaves the wheel without having transferred much of its momentum to the wheel. The loss is thus large. The amount of momentum given to the wheel being the amount lost by the water, it is evident, that when the water leaves the wheel rapidly, and thus retains much of its momentum, but a small amount is given to the wheel.

131. *In the flutter wheel, the loss is about five-sixths of the full effect of the water.*

This wheel is used with a high head, 10, 15, or 20 feet. The water issuing from an opening near the bottom of the flume, strikes the floats of the flutter wheel with great velocity and makes it revolve rapidly. As the water only transfers to the wheel a momentum, measured by the weight of the water multiplied by the velocity it loses, the momentum given is small.

In the overshot wheel which moves slowly, the water leaves the wheel with a small velocity, having transferred nearly all its power to the wheel. In the undershot, which moves more rapidly, the water leaves the wheel with more velocity, and thus transfers but a small portion of its force to the wheel. In the flutter wheel, which moves still more rapidly, the water retains a large portion of its velocity, and the momentum transferred is therefore very small.

In the first case the velocity of the wheel is small, but the mass in motion is large, making the momentum large. In the second the velocity is greater, but the mass being reduced more than the velocity is increased, the momentum is less. In the third case the velocity is large, but the mass being very small, the momentum is small.

132. *In the breast wheel, the loss of power is about one-half the full effect of the water.*

In this the water acts partly by its weight and partly by its impulse, and the loss is therefore between that of the overshot and undershot wheels.

133. *In the reaction wheels of the best kind, the loss is about the same as in the overshot.*

In these, the water commonly passes down a vertical column to the centre of a drum, then passes horizontally through the radii of this drum, and then escapes through openings on one side of these radii. The water escaping on one side of the radii, and pressing on the other, by its reaction forces the drum to revolve.

It is not best to have the water pass in straight lines from the centre to the rim of the drum, but in a spiral line bending in a direction opposite to that in which the drum revolves.

The advantage of these wheels is that they can move at high velocities with but little loss of power, and the drum may revolve under water with less resistance than other wheels.

134. *The expense of water power is usually much less than that of steam or animal power.*

A good dam may cost 1500 or 2000 dollars; this at a small annual repair of one or two hundred dollars will last ten or twelve years, even if constructed of wood. The annual cost for interest, depreciation, and repairs, will seldom reach one dollar per day; while a power equal to that of forty or fifty horses may be obtained from the water.

LECTURE XI.

COMMON ROADS.

135. *In laying out common roads, attention must be paid to the selection of the route, the acclivities, and the drainage.*

Of these the drainage is the most important, and the selection of the route the least.

136. *The first rule for the selection of the route is that it should be as short as possible.*

This lessens the cost of making the road, the quantity of land occupied by it, and the amount of friction to be overcome in passing from one point to another. It is proper however, to deviate more or less from a straight line to avoid a hill or a marsh, or to improve the grade of the road.

137. *All deviations from the direct route should be at small angles with it.*

If the angle made by the road with the direct route is small, the distance is very little increased. Thus, if the deviation were 12°, or 1 mile in 5, the length of the road would be increased only 2 miles in 100. In this case, if the distance between two places be 50 miles, the greatest deviation from the straight line would be 5 miles, but the whole length of the route would be increased only one mile. And universally, since the straight route is to the indirect route as the cosine of the deviation is to radius, and the cosine for small angles being nearly the same as radius, and for larger differing more and more, it is evident that the loss in distance will increase more rapidly than the angle of deviation increases.

138. *The first rule in regard to acclivities is, that in countries generally level, no rise over* 1 *in* 20 *should be allowed.*

If hills steeper than this should be met, they should be avoided, or cut down, or ascended by an indirect route, so that the rate of ascent should not exceed more than 1 in 20.

On such a road a horse can do nearly as well as on a level.

Friction is not increased, since the road is lengthened but a trifle. There is no loss from gravity, because on the descending grades the horse does not hold back, and the advantage received from gravity is equal to the loss on the ascending grades. The load may be as large as on a level road, for as the horse is rested on the descents, he can exert without fatigue an extra force on the ascents. The only loss is caused by the increase of force necessary to raise the horse's body up the acclivities, since it is about as difficult for him to move his body on the descending grades as it is on a level.

To express these forces in numbers, suppose a horse to draw a load of 2000 lbs. for three miles; first on a level road; then on a road ascending 1 in 20 for one mile, level for one mile, and then descending one in twenty for one mile. On the first, the weight to be overcome would be 100 lbs. for friction, and 125 lbs. to move forward the horse's body, or 225 lbs. for each one of the three miles. On the first mile of the second road the weight to be raised would be 100 lbs. for friction, 100 for gravity, 125 to move forward the horse's body, and $\frac{1}{20}$ of the weight of the horse's body to be lifted up the plane, which supposing him to weigh 1000 lbs. would be 50 lbs.; making the whole weight 100+100+125+50 or 375 lbs. on the first mile. On the second mile the weight would be 225 lbs. On the third mile, it would be 100—100+125 or 125 lbs. Thus on the level road the weight for the three miles would be 225×3 or 675 lbs.; on the undulating three miles, it would be 375+225+125 or 725 lbs.; the difference, 50 lbs, being caused by the necessity of lifting the horse's body up the inclined plane.

If, however, the road were steeper than 1 in 20, the loss in ascending could not be made up in descending, for the horse must now hold back; force must be exerted on the descending plane to resist gravity; the load must be diminished below what can be drawn on a level, else the horse would be strained and injured, or if not, still rendered unable, by excessive fatigue, from doing a full day's work. Besides this, it is difficult on steep ascents to keep the road-way in order, the accumulation of water in wet weather, and its rapid motion, washing away the soil, and making the road rough and uneven.

139. *In hilly or mountainous countries, no rise over* 1 *in* 12 *should be allowed.*

On such a road, the weight to be raised on the steepest part would be $W \div 20 + W \div 12 + 125 + H \div 12$, representing the weight of the horse's body by H. If the horse be suffered to exert any extra force on the steepest parts of the road, a proper load would be 1200 lbs. But if the road is made steeper, the exertion necessary to raise the horse's body up the ascents, and the double loss from holding back on the descents, reduce the load and the amount of work done very rapidly.

140. *If a steep hill is met, it may always be ascended by an indirect or zigzag route, so as to reduce the grade as much as may be desired.*

This will lengthen the route, increase the cost of the road, and also the friction of the wagons; but the gain from the increased load of the horse will more than compensate for these losses.

The hill may also be cut down, and the approaches to it filled up, but the cost of this is so considerable, that it cannot be done to any large extent for a common road.

141. *The injuries done by water, consist not only in its making the road-bed muddy, and thus increasing the resistance; but in its washing the soil away from the stones, and forming channels across the way, making it rough and uneven; and in its permitting the road-bed to freeze, which keeps it a long while rough and muddy.*

The losses from these sources being greater than from increasing the length of the route, or from having slight acclivities in the road, it is proper to go out of the direct route, and even to rise considerable ascents, to secure proper drainage.

142. *The road should avoid marshes, ground-springs, all wet places, the lowest parts of a valley, or of a mountain gorge.*

As it is difficult to drain such places as these, it is very desirable to avoid them. This can always be done in a valley or a mountain gorge, but for the others it may not always be possible. In this case, great attention must be paid to the drainage. Ditches should be dug at the side of the road; blind drains should be formed in the middle, filled with large stones and covered up with soil. Covered drains should lead from the ground-springs, and from the blind drains in the middle to the sides; and outlets should be made from the side ditches, to carry away the water at every practicable point. Should these methods be insufficient to make the road-bed dry, it should be raised by a suitable soil, so high as to drain itself into the side ditches. If this will not succeed, the wet soil should be covered with large stones or rails, or small trees, and these completely covered to a considerable depth by soil, so as to prevent the wood from decaying, and to make the way smooth and even. This covering with soil is very important; for the stones not only obstruct the progress of the vehicle, but injure it very much, and cause great discomfort to the traveler. The durability of the road is also very much prolonged.

143. *There should be ditches on both sides of the road usually; but when the ground falls off on one side, one is needed only for the upper side.*

If the water runs across the way, it is impossible to have a good road. The ditches are to prevent this and also to receive the rain water that falls on the road. Much of this runs off to the side, but some of it sinks into the road-bed and percolates under the ground to the side ditches.

The side ditches should be wide and deep enough to carry off the water; should have a fall of one foot in a hundred whenever practicable, so as to keep themselves open; and should be much broader at the top than at the bottom, lest their sides should fall in and obstruct the passage of the water. Their outlets should be numerous, especially on a long or steep declivity, so that they will not be overflowed during the heaviest shower.

144. *When the water must cross the road, it should be by a culvert, or under a bridge, or by a broad shallow sur-*

face-drain so constructed as not to become uneven by washing.

The culverts, though most expensive at first, are the best. By giving them a slight fall, they keep open, if sufficiently large to pass not only the water but the leaves and rubbish washed into them. The surface-drains are often paved.—Their inclination should be slight, not over six inches for a road of moderate breadth. They should be frequent on hills or long inclined planes, to assist in diverting the rain water off the road.

145. *When two inclined planes meet, an outlet for the water should be carefully made.*

In a soil of pure sand, this is not important. In fact the water is sometimes intentionally obstructed in this case, so that the materials carried down by the water should be deposited, and fill up the depression. But if the soil is of clay, or contains a portion of clay, an outlet must be carefully provided, else the water is retained, and a muddy place formed in the road.

146. *The cross section of the road should be elevated in the middle* 5 *or* 6 *inches, to a breadth of* 20 *feet.*

This is necessary not only to carry off the rain-water, but to give to the water that has sunk into the ground a better chance to escape to the side ditches.

147. *It is best to repair roads frequently, and after wet weather.*

By constant attention, the road can be kept all the while good at a less cost, than when the repairs are made only once or twice a year. If the road-bed is moist, the soil for repairing can be dug up more easily, and it will sooner consolidate and unite with the old road.

148. *The best material for repairs is a mixture of clay and sand, in which the clay predominates.*

A vegetable mould is very objectionable; because it is spongy, and absorbs and retains moisture. Sand is too soft and yielding. Clay is tough when wet, and does not dry readily. Stones make the road-way too rough, unless they are very small, about an inch cube, and of uniform size.—Rounded gravel is too yielding, both to the feet of the horses and the wheels of the wagons. But a soil which contains a proper proportion of sand and clay is firm and hard, throws off the rain water well, drys rapidly, and forms a smooth and durable road.

LECTURE XII.

COMMON ARTIFICIAL ROADS.

149. *The Roman Military Roads were the earliest of any extent, where a superstructure was placed on the ground to form the road-bed.*

These centered at Rome, and led thence to every part of the Empire; their total length being more than 50,000 miles. Though made principally for the passage of soldiers and pack-horses with the baggage of their armies, light carriages for travellers were also used on them. They were of the most substantial kind, so that not only their ruins are yet traced in Italy, but many portions of them are still travelled on at the present time. They were constructed of stones, large in size and durable in material, bound together with a mortar or cement of the best kind, two or three feet deep, and covered with flag.stones so as to make them smooth and pleasant.

These would be too costly for modern use; and our heavy wagons would disarrange the pavements so as to introduce water, and its freezing would break up the road.

150. *The turnpike road consists of a road-bed made of broken stone,* 10 *or* 15 *inches deep.*

Of these 30 or 40 thousand miles have been built in England, and more than 10000 miles in the United States. Their cost in this country has been from 5 to 10 thousand dollars per mile, but though of great advantage to the country through which they pass, they have seldom been pro-

7

fitable to the stock holders. Since the introduction of railroads, new turnpikes have been very few.

Before laying down the broken stone, the route is more carefully selected than for common roads, the acclivities lessened by cuttings and embankments, and the road-bed thoroughly drained. The black vegetable mould is removed from the surface.

If the sub-soil is of fine sand, large flat stones are laid down as a foundation to prevent the broken stone from working down into the sand and disappearing entirely. If the base is of clay or partly of clay, these large stones should not be used. If the base is marshy, flag-stones or small trees should form the foundation for the broken stone. If a solid rock comes to the surface, it is well to cover this with soil; else the broken stone laid on this are easily crushed by the wagons, and also fail to become firm and consolidated.

The stones should be of the hardest and toughest kind, so as to be durable. They should be small enough to pass through a ring $2\frac{1}{2}$ inches in diameter in their longest direction, else they would make the way rough and become obstructions to the wheels. They should not be, however, very small, else they would not bind together. They should be angular and not round like gravel, or they would not form a firm hard base to support the wheel and turn off the rain-water that falls on the road.

Hard granite or tough limestone, basalt, trap, and a hard clay freestone are proper kinds of rock for the broken stone. Common granite or limestone is too soft; so are sand-stone and slate usually; quartz and flint are too brittle.

This mass of broken stone is not covered with clay or soil; but, after it is used a short time, forms of itself a smooth hard dry road-bed almost impervious to water and uninjured by frost or wet weather.

151. *The Macadamised road differs from the turnpike, mainly in the small size of the broken stone.*

The Cumberland road built by the United States Government, and leading from the Potomac across the Ohio at Wheeling and thence westward towards St. Louis, is of this kind.

Many of the English roads are Macadamised ; but in the United States they are found only in the neighborhood of the large cities. Their cost is from 10 to 20,000 dollars per mile. They are an excellent and pleasant road, but their cost forbids their general introduction.

The size of the stones is about a cubic inch ; the greatest length in any direction being two inches, or the heaviest being four ounces. Hard tough angular stones of this size will after a short use form a smooth compact surface through which water will not penetrate.

152. *The plank road is made of planks two or three inches thick, laid across the road, on longitudinal sleepers* 10 *or* 12 *inches wide.*

These have been used in Russia for a long time ; they were introduced into Canada in 1840 ; more recently they have been constructed very largely in New York and to some extent in other Northern states ; the amount yet built in the South is very small.

Before laying down the sleepers, the route is marked out with much care, and thoroughly drained. As friction even for common waggons is reduced to one thirtieth on these roads, 1 in 30 is the maximum grade that should be allowed, so that the horse may be able, without straining, to take, on the acclivities, his full load on a level.

The sleepers should be full 12 inches wide so as to have a broad bearing surface on the ground. Two are enough, if the road is a single track ; for which eight feet is the proper width. The two sleepers should be one foot from the end of the planks, so that the distance between them would be four feet. One should be about an inch higher than the other, so as to give the planks a cross slope to carry off the rain water. For a double track four sleepers are necessary, and plank sixteen feet long. The sleepers must be buried in the ground, so that the plank shall be supported their whole length by the earth ; and this must be carefully rammed under them, to secure a continuous bearing, or else the plank will decay very rapidly.

153. *The cost of plank roads is very small; between one and two thousand dollars per mile.*

The two rows of sleepers 12 inches by 4, a mile long, will contain 2X4X5280 or 42000 feet. The plank, if two inches thick, will contain 8X2X5280 or 84000 feet. And both at $8 per thousand will cost $1008. For the grading and preparation of the road-bed, from 300 to 800 dollars will be required. For putting down the superstructure $200 would be sufficient. So that the whole cost would not exceed 1500 to 2000 dollars per mile. When lumber is cheap and the route favorable, so as to require but little grading, the cost is still less.

154. *The durability of plank roads depends on the climate, and the amount and character of the freight on them.*

In cold countries, as in Russia or Canada, they would last ten years before rotting; in New York 7 or 8 years; in the South not more than 4 or 5.

Sometimes the amount of travel and of freight is so large, that the planks are worn out before they rot; but that is always a favorable circumstance, since the tolls will then always pay handsome dividends to the stockholders.

155. *Plank roads are suited for those localities where a good natural road cannot be obtained.*

In sandy or marshy districts the saving is very great, not only in the increased load of the horse, but in the rapid passage of carriages. So in prairie lands, where the deep tough mud makes the roads almost impassable in winter. So also, in Northern countries, where the ground becomes frozen for two or three feet below the surface, and remains for a long while in the spring thawing and freezing, making the road rough and muddy to a great depth.

156. *The load of a horse on an ordinary plank road is not less than* 2000 *lbs.*

If the grades were very good, rising one in 30 or one in 40, the load would be still larger. But where the grade is one in 20, the friction 2000 lbs. is only 66 and gravity 100 lbs. So that the average weight to be raised on the level and the steepest grade is only 116 lbs. which is less than the power of an ordinary horse. If now the muddy or rough common road would permit only a load of 7 or 800 lbs., the saving would authorise the payment of 75 cents per ton per day in the form of tolls, since two horses would do the work of five.

The saving of time and the increase of comfort to the traveller would be still more marked and important.

157. *If a plank road should cost* $1500 *per mile and last five years*, 100 *loaded horses should pass per day to render it profitable.*

One cent per horse per mile is as much as could be collected for toll. In muddy weather, 2 horses on the plank-road would do the work of 5 on the common road. The 4000 lbs. would thus require three horses less. Counting this saving at $1.50 per day, it would give 7½ cents per mile or 3¾ cents per horse. But when the common roads were not much out of order, the saving would be less; and in neither case must the whole saving be charged for toll, or no inducement would be offered to the wagoner to use the plank road. For passengers the toll might be 2 cents per mile per horse, as their comfort would be much increased as well as that of their horses. For a road 50 miles long, one fifth of the horses being for pleasure carriages, the receipts for 100 horses would be (80+20×2)50 or $60 per day. For the year they would be 60×365 or $21900. Deducting from this $900 for six toll-collectors, and $50 per mile for repairs, the net receipts will be $18500. The cost of the road being 50×1500 or $75000, the receipts would make a dividend of 25 per cent. And this amount is needed, so as to give the stockholders 7 per cent, and return them their capital in five years.

158. *Streets are paved with small round boulder stones of quartz, or with blocks of granite, or with cast iron, or with a mixture of asphaltum and chips of stone, and sometimes with blocks of wood.*

The first kind of pavement is the most common. It is cheap, very durable, easily laid down and taken up, and forms a good foot-hold for the horses. But it is rough, noisy, and disagreeable to the passengers.

The blocks of granite have recently been introduced in London and Paris, and to some extent in our Northern cities. This pavement is smooth, very durable, and very pleasant. It is expensive and often becomes so smooth that the horses slip and fall on it. As the blocks are squared and fitted close to each other, the rain-water cannot get under it and soften the base, so as to make the blocks sink unequally and the road become uneven.

Sometimes the blocks are 3 or 4 or 5 feet long and laid in rows about 5 feet apart, so that the wheels may roll in them; while the space between is filled with small boulders or with broken stone, to form a good foot-hold for the horses. Two or three of these rows are laid, so as to accommodate the vehicles passing in both directions. This forms an admirable road, but does not suit well for cities, where so many vehicles are passing and meeting continually.

Plates of cast iron have been tried for pavements, but though firm, smooth and durable, they soon become too smooth for the horses, however rough they may be when first laid down.

Asphaltum is a kind of mineral coal which being melted and mixed with small chippings of hard stone, forms a cheap cement, with which a road-bed and pavements are sometimes made. This forms a good road, but wears unequally, and is not very durable.

Blocks of wood cut agross the grain, and set up on the ends, have been used for pavements. These make a very smooth, firm and cheap road-bed for a short time; but however carefully they are joined, the water will at some places get between them and rot the wood. The decay once begun progresses rapidly by opening the seam and admitting more and more water. If the rot could be prevented they would form a durable road, because the wheels rub against the ends of the grain, and therefore wear it slowly.

Sometimes a McAdamised way of broken stone is used in cities. But this wears rapidly and becomes very dusty, and cannot be taken up readily, when it is necessary to lay down or repair the water or gas pipes under the streets.

LECTURE XIII.

HISTORY OF RAILROADS.

159. *A Rail Road is one on which the carriages roll on a superstructure of stone, wood, or iron.*

Among the ancients the immense masses of rock used in the public buildings were drawn from the quarries on a way made of blocks of stone, and these may be regarded as the first railroads ever constructed. Wooden ways were used at Newcastle in England, early in the 17th century, for transporting coal from the mines to the river, a mile or two distant. These were constructed by pinning down, lengthwise along the road, wooden sills 6 or 8 inches square, on cross pieces of about the same size laid 2 or 3 feet apart. By these, the load of the horse was more than doubled, being increased from 17 to 42 cwt. As there were many teams carrying these heavy loads, the wood wore away very rapidly and required to be replaced in a year or two, long before it had rotted. For convenience of replacing, a thick plank was sometimes pinned on the sills that were laid in the direction of the road. These planks were renewed from time to time, while the under rails and cross-ties were not taken up for 8 or 10 years, when from their complete decay they would no longer answer the purpose. These wooden roads continued in use for 150 years, before iron was substituted for the wooden rails, the first use of iron being about the year 1767. The wooden roads were generally used till about the year 1800, and from the cheapness of wood in the United States they continued to be used here still later. It is now found, that even for temporary purposes the iron road is always best. If the amount of freight will authorise the construction of a wooden track, the additional outlay for iron will be more than compensated by the decreased cost of transportation.

160. *The modern railroad, for the purpose of travel and general transportation, was not introduced until* 1830.

A great number of short iron roads 2 or 3 miles long, and in a few cases 8 or 9 miles long, were used in the coal districts in Great Britain, at the beginning of the present century; and in 1800 the Surrey Railroad leading from London southward through the county of Surrey, was chartered for the general purposes of trade. It was 18 miles long, and was finished in 1806. It was not successful or profitable to the stockholders. Several Railroads, 20 or 30 miles long, were constructed between this time and 1830, with the intention of carrying passengers and general merchandise in part, but their main object was to transport coal and iron.—Horses were generally employed on them, but in 1811 the locomotive was introduced. In 1816 Stephenson improved the locomotive of Trevithick and Vivian so that its use became more general; but it was at low velocities of 3 or 4 miles per hour. Not until 1830, when the Liverpool and Manchester Railroad was opened, did the locomotive obtain such velocity and power, that it could compete with the stage coach for passengers and with other modes of conveyance for merchandise. Before this time, no rail road was built on the continent of Europe or America, except for short distances, from mines or quarries, for the transportation of coal, iron, or stone.

161. *From* 1830 *forwards, Rail Roads have been every where introduced with great rapidity and success.*

In 1830 there were not more than 500 miles of Rail-way in Europe and America. In 1840 there were 1000 miles in Great Britain alone; and 7000 at the end of 1852. The cost of these roads having been about $170000 per mile, the amount expended on them has reached the enormous sum of 1200 millions of dollars. So rapid an increase shows that the investment must have been as profitable to the stockholders as it was beneficial to the public.

In France, the progress has been slower and the stock less productive. In 1830, there were no roads except in the mineral districts. In 1840, the number of miles opened for passengers was less than 100. At the beginning of 1853 the amount was 2500 miles. The cost of these roads has been about $120000 per mile, and the capital invested 300 millions of dollars.

In Belgium, there were no railways in 1830; in 1840, there were 200 miles in operation; and at the beginning of 1853, they reached 500 miles. Their cost has been about $60000 per mile, and the capital invested 30 millions.—They have been profitable and of great advantage to the country.

In the German states, including Prussia and Austria, there were at the beginning of 1853 about 5000 miles, constructed at a cost of $60000 per mile, involving an expenditure of 300 millions of capital. These have been mostly built since 1840 and have been profitable and advantageous.

In Russia, about 500 miles were finished at the beginning of 1853, at a cost of $60000 per mile, but the lines were principally built by the government and their receipts and expenses have not been made known.

In Portugal, Spain, Italy, Holland, Switzerland, Turkey, and Denmark, Rail Roads have been but little introduced; not over 500 miles being built in all these countries.

In the United States, the first iron Rail Road was the Quincy, near Boston, 3 miles long and built in 1826. The next was the Lehigh in Pennsylvania, 9 miles long and built in 1827. These were for transporting granite and coal. In 1828 three long lines were commenced, for the transportation of merchandise and travelers. Of these, the South Carolina railroad from Charleston to Hamburg was completed in 1833; the Pennsylvania road from Philadelphia to the Susquehanna in 1835; and the Baltimore and Ohio was not opened, the whole way through, until 1852. The number of miles in operation on the first of January in

the years	1835	1840	1845	1850	1851	1852	1853,
was	900	2200	4500	7500	9000	11000	13500,

thus doubling every five years; and their present rate of progress is fully as rapid as at any former period. Their cost has been about $30000 per mile, making the whole outlay 400 millions. A few of the lines have been unprofitable, but the great majority have paid handsome dividends on the amount invested in their construction, besides being of immense benefit in developing the resources and increasing the wealth of our country.

162. *The extent of Rail Roads in the United States exceeds that of any other country, and soon it will exceed that of all other countries put together.*

The amount in England increased in the last five years only 2000 miles; in all the other countries of Europe, the increase has been about the same amount; while in the United States the number of miles completed has advanced in the same time from 5700 to 13500 miles. The lines now in progress authorise us to expect that 20000 miles will be in operation at the beginning of 1855; while in no other country excepting France is there much prospect of a rapid increase. The present amount in Europe, which is 16000 miles, will not probably be as large as 20000 at the beginning of 1855.

163. *The railroads of the United States, though far less costly than those abroad, are but little inferior.*

In England the cost of obtaining charters from Parliament has been considerable; the right of way and the lands for depots have required immense sums: tunnels have been numerous; handsome station houses have been built, and much money has been wasted in making the road nearly level. Many are supplied with a double track.

In France, the Government has had much to do in constructing the roads, and its expenditures are always wasteful and extravagant.

In the other countries of Europe, the cost has been but little above ours, and that excess is principally due to the utlay for land.

Some of our roads have been laid with light iron, some are poorly supplied with engines and cars, with depots and machine-shops; but the great majority have heavy iron, are well equipped, and but little inferior to the European lines.

164. *Among the several states of the Union, New York is first in the amount of her railroads, and then follow next in order, Ohio, Pennsylvania, Massachusetts, and Georgia.*

The amount in N. York is 2150 miles, and the principal lines are from N. York to Dunkirk on Lake Erie; and from N. York to Buffalo through Albany. The greater part of these roads have been very profitable.

In Ohio the amount is 1400 miles. The principal lines are from Cincinnati to Sandusky; and from Cincinnati to Cleaveland through Columbus. Other routes, along Lake Erie to connect with the N. York lines; across the middle of the state to connect with the Pennsylvania roads; and along the Southern part of the State, to connect with the Baltimore and Ohio railroad, are partly open and will soon be completed. These have been built cheaply and have been very profitable.

In Pennsylvania the number of miles is 1250. The principal lines are from Philadelphia to Ohio through Harrisburg and Pittsburg; from Philadelphia to the coal districts up the Schuylkill; from Philadelphia towards Baltimore, and towards N. York. These roads have been built at great expense and but few have made a good return for the money invested in them.

In Massachusetts the amount opened for travel is 1150 miles. The principal routes are from Boston, northward towards Maine; west of north to New Hampshire; north of west to Vermont; westward to Albany; southwest towards N. York; and southeast to several points on the coast.—This State is better supplied with railroads in proportion to its size and population than any other in the Union. They have been built at great expense, on account of the character of the country; but almost all have been well managed and profitable.

Georgia, though the ninth State in population, is the fifth

in the number of her railroads. The principal routes are from Savannah northwest to Tennessee through Macon and Atlanta; and from Augusta westward towards Alabama through Atlanta and Lagrange. From the first, branches lead towards Augusta, Eatonton, Oglethorpe, Rome, and Knoxville in Tennessee; and from the second, to Warrenton and to Athens. The length of all is over 900 miles. They have been built very cheaply, on favorable routes, and have all been profitable except the State Road above Atlanta.

165. *After these States come next in order Indiana, Virginia, Connecticut and South Carolina.*

In Indiana the main lines are from Terre Haute, eastward through Indianapolis towards Ohio; from Madison on the Ohio river northwest through Indianapolis towards Chicago on lake Michigan. The number of miles now completed is 750; but the new routes in progress are so numerous, that she will soon rank next after Pennsylvania in the amount of her railroads.

In Virginia the principal route is from the Potomac through Richmond to Weldon. The whole amount in the State is about 700 miles.

The road first built in South Carolina, was from Charleston northwest to Hamburg. From Branchville on this road a route runs northward through Columbia towards Charlotte in N. Carolina. From this, a line runs northeast to Camden; and from this a line, eastward through Manchester towards Wilmington. Another route starts from Columbia northwest towards Greenville. The whole amount now in operation is about 650 miles. Their cost has been higher than in Georgia. The older roads have however been profitable; while the rest have been too recently in operation to enable us to form an opinion of them in this respect.

166. *Of the other States, those east of Ohio and South Carolina are well supplied with railroads, and most of the rest are making rapid progress in their construction.*

This progress is especially true in Alabama, Tennessee and Illinois, though the amount now completed in these states is small.

167. *The rapidity with which capital has been invested in these enterprises is unequalled in the history of the world.*

The annual gross receipts from the 2300 millions invested in railroads in Europe and the United States, is more than 250 millions. This exceeds the annual value of the cotton raised throughout the whole world. It also exceeds the whole whole of the iron produced. These two interests have made more rapid progress than any other branch of industry; but their growth has been for a longer period, and the magnitude which they have attained is less than the Rail Road interest.

168. *This rapid progress of railroads has been due mainly to the invention of the Locomotive.*

Without this, they must have been confinedto those mineral districts where canals could not be constructed, and to the more important routes of travel and transportation, where large and valuable freights demanded rapid movements. Their progress commenced with the success of the Locomotive, and without it there is no doubt that but few would have been profitable. Its rapidity and regularity secures to the railroad the transit of passengers and the lighter goods, while its cheapness excludes the competition of horse power for heavier articles.

LECTURE XIV.

RAIL ROADS.

169. *The first iron rails used for Rail Roads were of cast iron; but since* 1830 *wrought iron is exclusively employed.*

Cast iron was preferred to the wrought, because it was cheaper, harder and not liable to rust in the open air. The rusting, however, is slight whichever kind is used, as the top surface is kept smooth and polished by constant rubbing. The toughness of the wrought iron makes it as durable as the cast, under the grinding action of the wheels, although it is much softer. Since the introduction of the locomotive with its great weight and high velocities, cast iron has been entirely abandoned, as it is brittle under heavy blows, and a broken rail might cause serious accidents. The wrought or rolled rail was introduced in 1808, but since 1830 its use has been universal.

170. *The successive forms that have been used for rails, have been the heavy rectangular bar, the flange, the plate, the edge, the inverted* ⊥, *the* H, *the inverted* ∩ *or bridge, and the compound rail.*

The heavy bar of cast iron was first used instead of the wooden sleepers; but as the metal was brittle and the loads immense, the rails broke frequently.

To insure strength, the shape was altered, without any change in the amount of iron. The same material was made deep and thin, since the strength increases as the square of the depth. Hence, the edge rail. The breadth at the top was kept $2\frac{1}{2}$ inches, as less would cut into the wheels; but this breadth was retained only an inch from the top, when it was reduced to one inch, and this thickness continued for the whole depth of the rail. Fig. 16.

This shape of the rail is not, however, the best for strength. When a bar is supported at two ends, and sustains a weight resting on the middle, the strain is mostly at the top and at the bottom. The bar yields by the crushing of the atoms at the top, or the tearing apart of those at the bottom, the strain on the middle being very slight. Hence, more of the metal was distributed at the bottom, and thus the ⊥ and the H rail were introduced. Figs. 17 and 18.

The inverted ∩ (fig. 19) was introduced for the same reasons. It has a broader bearing surface on the base than the ⊥ rail, as the ⊥ is broader than the H.

Of these three forms, the ⊥, if well shaped, is the best. The upper broad part must be about an inch deep before it begins to narrow, or the wheels will crush and tear off the projecting part, especially on the curves, where the conical wheels present a small bearing surface. The breadth at the bottom not only gives strength, but prevents cutting into the wood below. The shape is the most favorable disposition that can be made of the material. The ∩ is not so strong with the same amount of iron. The H has not sufficient breadth of base, and cannot be fastened so well to the wood and to the chairs.

To lessen the amount of iron, a plate rail resting on a continuous bearing of wood was introduced. This being weak, and only $2\frac{1}{2}$ inches wide cut into the wood, which was of irregular hardness on account of knots and for other reasons, the rail became bent and loose from the wood, and rising at the end, formed what was called snake-heads. These were very dangerous, especially for heavy loads and high velocities. The wood also required frequent repairs. This rail was thus found in the end to be more expensive than the heavy ⊥ or the ∩, so that it is now almost every where abandoned.

To aid in giving strength to the flat rail, a flange was added at the side, sometimes turning upwards, and sometimes downwards. This increased the stiffness, but was not the best use of the material for this purpose; and both forms of this flange rail are now no longer employed.

Whatever form of rail be adopted, the line is always weak at the points where two rails meet. They cannot be welded or pinned together, or firmly united to an iron base or chair, because of the expansion and contraction of the rails by heat and cold, as the change of temperature from zero up to 135°, which is reached under the hot sun, will alter the length of a 20 feet rail $\frac{2}{10}$ of an inch. As they cannot be united firmly, it is difficult to keep the joint even, so as to prevent one rail from rising above the other or from being bent to the right or left. This has led to the compound rail. This has the shape of the common ⊥ cut into two parts by a vertical plane running from end to end. The joint on the one half is placed opposite the middle of the other half, so that every where along the line the wheels are supported by half the rail. The two halves are united together by a projection on the side of one, fitting into a depression on the side of the other, thus forming a single mass to support the weight. They are farther united by pins or rivets driven through the two halves. If there was only one pin through the middle of each half, it would not at all prevent the expansion by changes of temperature. If there were two or more, they would interfere with it between the rivets, but the parts between the rivets and the ends would yet be free. The expansion between the rivets, however, being small, it has been found, that by giving them a little play, they will not be broken by the expansion of the bars. This compound rail has been but recently introduced, is more expansive than the ordinary ⊥, and has not yet secured general confidence; but the trial of it both in New York and Pennsylvania has been quite satisfactory. Should it succeed, it would increase very much the smoothness and comfort of the road, cause a great saving in repairs to the engines and cars and road-bed, and remove entirely those obstructions at the joints which no art or skill seems able to prevent with the common rail.

171. *Chairs at the joints are necessary to give strength to the line and unite the rails.*

Without them the rails would cut into the wood unequally and no longer be in the same level; the cross-ties, having wheels first resting on one side and then on the other, would become tilted and thus increase the obstacle at the joints; nor would the two rails remain in the same line.

They are usually of cast iron, because it is cheaper than wrought. They are broad, so as to give a large bearing surface on the cross-ties. They have cheeks on each side to confine the two rails in a single line. Sometimes the cheeks are high so that two rivets are made to pass through the cheeks and the two rails; but this plan does not allow for expansion, even if the rivets have some play. Sometimes an iron or a wooden wedge is driven between the high cheeks and the hollow at the side of the ⊥ rail. This fastening is very good. If the cheeks are low, spikes are driven through the base of the ⊥ and the chair into the wood below. If the iron rail has not a broad base, a chair is often put under it at each cross-tie.

172. *The rails should be* 18 *or* 20 *feet long, and weigh* 50 *or* 60 *lbs. to the yard.*

The greater the length the better; because the weakness and obstructions at the joints are less numerous. As the upper surface must be about 2½ inches broad, it would require a weight of 55 lbs. to the yard, to give a depth of 3 inches, a breadth at the bottom of 3½ inches, and a thickness in the middle of 1 inch.

173. *The rails in use range from* 45 *to* 75 *lbs. The guage or breadth between the inner sides of the rails is commonly* 4 *feet* 8½ *inches. On the Southern roads it is five feet, and on some few, North and South, it is still wider.*

The broad guage is a little more expensive, having more difference between the length of the inner and outer track, and therefore more slipping of the wheels. The axles of the cars must be stronger and heavier, on account of their increased length. But as the base is broader and the centre of gavity lower for the same load, the train is more steady and comfortable. The locomotive can be made so as to have more power and more velocity by an increased breadth of fire-box and flues, and therefore a greater ability to generate steam.

Were not the narrow guage generally adopted, a width of 5½ or 6 feet would no doubt be preferred. As it is, however, often very desirable, to pass from one road to another without unloading freight or baggage, a break in the guage is very objectionable. New roads are therefore built of the same width as the old ones with which they are connected.

174. *The superstructure on which the rails rest should be of wood, and not of stone.*

In the earlier roads, the iron was made to rest on stone blocks or sills, with the design of giving greater firmness to the track; but as the ground, on which the blocks or sills rested, yielded unequally, the rails soon became uneven, and the stiff unbending masses of rock jarred and injured the locomotive and the cars, and caused much discomfort to the passengers. These have, therefore, been entirely abandoned. If the cross-ties are of stone, these objections are not so serious, but still they exist.

175. *The best form of superstructure is a longitudinal sill resting on cross-ties near each other.*

A distance of 4 or 5 feet between the cross-ties was formerly common; but in the best recent roads, this is reduced to 2½ or 3 from centre to centre. As this gives a greater bearing surface, the ground is less liable to yield unequally and make the track uneven. A string-piece of wood forming a continuous support to the rail, and resting on the cross-ties, is better than to have the rails supported by the cross-ties alone. As wood is very cheap in our country, the nearness of the sills and the additional string-piece will add very little to the cost of the road. To put the cross-ties 2½ feet apart instead of 4, would increase the expense in the South only about $300 per mile, and the string-pieces would add about $200 more; and these would be small items in the cost of the road.

The longitudinal sill is let down into the cross-ties, and wedged in its seat, to prevent the spreading of the track by the action of the flanges of the wheels. The rails are confined to the string-piece by numerous spikes driven through the base into the wood below.

Sometimes the cross-ties rest on longitudinal mud-sills to increase the firmness and evenness of the road. In the North, a trench is dug 2 or 3 feet deep under the cross-ties, and filled with small broken stones. The object of this is to prevent the injury from frost. If the cross-ties rested on the ground, the water would get under them and freeze in the winter, and then by expanding disarrange the whole superstructure. This is expensive but indispensable in cold climates.

On some roads, both in England and America, a still greater amount of wood is used. A series of cross-ties is laid down, making an angle of about 45° with the line. Across these are laid another set at right angles to the first, forming a kind of lattice work. Each set is placed so near together, that they cross each other at three places. Notches are cut in both at each crossing, so that the bottom surfaces are all in the same level. A longitudinal sill is then placed on the top of this lattice track, to which the rail is fastened. This plan increases the cost of the road slightly, but the saving in the repairs of the engines and cars is considerable, on account of the evenness of the track; and if the business on the road is large, this saving will soon repay the increased cost of the superstructure.

176. *The outer track on a curve should be a little higher than the inner.*

The object of this is to counteract the tendency to fly off in a tangent to the curve. The downward sliding of the train towards the inner rail should balance the centrifugal motion towards the outer rail.

The centrifugal force increases with the velocity, so that this cannot be balanced for all velocities. It is usual to compensate for it at the higher velocities, as the resistance on the curves is then much the greatest.

To estimate the increased height to be given to the outer rail, consider that the centrifugal force is the versed-sine of the arc described, and therefore equals $A^2 \div 2R$, representing by A and R the length of the arc and its radius. That is, if the train have a velocity of 20 miles per hour or $28\frac{2}{3}$ feet per second, and the curve have 1000 feet radius, the centrifugal force $=28\frac{2}{3}^2 \div 2000$ or $\frac{4}{10}$ of a foot in one second. Now we must consider what must be the inclination of the track so that the cars would fall on it $\frac{4}{10}$ of a foot per second. The formula for this is $S=mH \div L$. Here $S=\frac{4}{10}$ and $L=5$ feet for the Georgia guage; hence $H=1\frac{1}{2}$ inches. And this is the height of the outer rail above the inner for this radius and velocity.

177. *Moderate grades are of great importance in laying out a route for a Railroad.*

If they are less than 22 feet in a mile, they are but slightly objectionable; especially if they are short, and a rising succeeds to a falling grade. The load may be nearly as great as on a level, as the steam will accumulate on the descents to be used on the ascents.

If the grade is 30 feet, the disadvantage is slight; but when it reaches 40 or 50 feet, the load is much lessened.—At still higher grades, the efficiency of the locomotive is reduced to one-fourth or one-fifth of what it can do on a level.

If the grade is generally as low as 20 or 30 feet in a mile, the route may be much lengthened, or a heavy cutting encountered, to bring a 40 or 50 feet grade down to the usual limit. In like manner for other grades.

178. *A steep grade of 100 feet or upwards was formerly overcome by a stationary engine, but now these are always avoided, by lengthening the road, by deep cutting, or by tunnelling.*

On the South Carolina road, and on the Pennsylvania road, built many years ago, when the locomotive was quite inferior to what it now is, stationary power was used; but the steep grades on these roads have since been avoided at great expense, by lengthening the road.

The stationary engine draws up the train by turning a large cylinder or drum at the top of the plane, and thus winding up a rope, attached to the cars. These ropes, whether made of hemp or iron wire, often break and become the cause of serious accidents. As they draw up the load slowly, and by parts, they cause delays and loss of time. They are also very expensive, because they carry the load but a short distance, and act only for a short time. On account of these delays, accidents, and expenses, it is better to lengthen the road several miles, and to submit to large additional outlays, rather than have a single one of these inclined planes.

179. *The cost of the Railroads in the Southern and Northwestern States is from* $10 *to* $20000 *per mile; in the Middle and Eastern States from* $20 *to* $50000.

From the Carolinas to the Mississippi, and from the Ohio to the Lakes, the country is so nearly level that the grading of a road has seldom exceeded $5000 per mile. The superstructure, including the laying it down, is limited at $2000 per mile. The heavy iron, including the chairs and spikes, counting the price at $50 per ton, would require $6000. The right of way, depots, water-stations, workshops, engines, cars,

&c. &c., may be put at $5000 more. Thus the whole cost of a good road, well equipped, would amount to $18000 per mile. In the mountainous regions of the Southern, Middle and Eastern States, the cost of excavation and embankment, of cutting in rock, of tunnelling and bridging, has increased the expense of construction to 30, 40 and even $50000 per mile. In some places the right of way, a double track, an unfavorable route, and the effort to make the track very nearly level, have raised the cost to over $50000; and on one road, viz: the Reading, to $160000 per mile.

LECTURE XV.

IMPROVEMENT OF RIVERS.

180. *If the navigation of rivers is interrupted by sand-bars, their removal is attended with great difficulty and expense.*

When the effort is made to remove them by dredging, that is by attaching a plough or a scraper to a boat which is driven by the current or by a steam engine, the bar may be temporarily removed, but the channel is soon re-filled by the sand brought down by the current.

If wing-dams are built out from the shore to throw the current to the other side, so that the large volume of water passing rapidly may make and keep open a channel, the effect extends but a small distance down the stream. If other wing-dams are built to continue this channel, the expense becomes very great. Or if a wall is built up and down the stream from the end of the first wing-dam to confine the current for a longer distance, the floods and drift-wood of the next winter may break away the dam or wall, and form the main channel at a new place, and thus render the former outlays entirely useless.

Whatever plan be adopted, great expense is always involved, while the advantage received is always small.

181. *When the channel of a river is interrupted by rocks, it may be opened by blasting the rocks and then removing them.*

If the rocks are loose and exposed because the water has washed away the soil around them, their removal is easy and usually of great advantage.

If a narrow ledge runs across the stream, forming a ripple or a fall, its removal by blasting is attended with greater expense, especially as the channel will often have to be opened for a considerable distance.

But if the ripple or fall extends down the stream even for a short distance, the cost of removal will be very great. The expense of blasting, the high wages of hands working in the water, and the length of the channel that has to be opened involves so large an outlay that it is seldom repaid by the advantage that is gained.

182. *When the navigation of a river is interrupted by snags, sawyers, water-logged timber, rafts, or other obstructions of wood, they can generally be removed to advantage.*

These are dragged out of their place by the force of steam, or of a descending boat, then sawed into pieces, and removed. Sometimes, they become partly covered with sand, and the force and labor required to displace them is increased. But in all cases they are foreign obstructions, interfering very much with the navigation, and usually removed at a moderate expense; so that the advantage gained more than balances the outlay incurred.

183. *When the fall is considerable or extends for a long distance, the stream is made navigable by dams or locks.*

The dam is placed at the bottom of the falls, and blacks the water so as to deepen the channel above. If it is desired to pass the boats only in one direction, a narrow opening is left in the dam through which the boat may pass. Sometimes the openings in the dam are supplied with gates to retain the water better. Sometimes they are supplied with locks.

184. *A lock is a chamber, large enough to contain the lar-*

gest boats on the river, connecting with an upper and lower level of water by gates, and used to raise and lower boats from one level to another.

It may be placed in the dam itself near the shore, or in the bank at the side. The gates are double, turn on vertical hinges, meet at an obtuse angle, and open up the stream, so that they are kept closely shut by the pressure of the water.—Near the bottom of each of the four gates are valves about a foot square. The upper beam of the gates projects beyond the hinges, and is made very heavy, so as to balance the weight of the gate, and form a lever by which they may be easily opened.

If a boat is to be passed upwards, the valves in the lower gates are opened, and the water runs out of the chamber, until it is on the same level as the water below. The lower gates are then opened, the boat floated into the lock, and the lower gates and valves closed. When the boat is thus confined in the lock, the valves in the upper gates are opened, the water enters and gradually raises the boat until it is as high as the water above, when the upper gates are opened and the boat floated out on the upper level. In like manner, the boat may be transferred from the upper to the lower level.

185. *Locks are usually made of cut stone, but sometimes of wood or of brick.*

They are built very substantially, on account of the great pressure of the water. Their depth is seldom over 12 feet, usually 8 or 10. If a greater fall than 12 feet is to be overcome, two or more locks are commonly made. The largest will pass a boat through in 8 or 10 minutes, so that very little time is lost. If used to pass boats drawn by two horses, they are commonly 100 feet long and 12 feet wide. For larger boats, or for steamboats, their size is increased.

186. *The dams, whether built of wood or stone, should have a base three or four times greater than their height.*

In building a dam of wood, it is usual to lay across the stream two rows of sills, with a distance between them three or four times the height of the dam. Upright posts are then raised on the lower sills. The sills and posts are all now united firmly together, forming a triangle. On the upper face of this, dry pine planks two inches thick are laid; and above the upper row of sills a piling of plank is driven into the soil for a great depth, or until it meets the rock below. If it reaches the rock, it must be made to fit it well by cutting the end to the piling to a proper shape.

The strength of this form of dam is very considerable.—The downward pressure of the water resting on the dam helps to hold it in its place; while the bracing of the sills and the facing plank bind it together, and prevents it moving downward with the current.

If the inclined plane had a base only double its length, the vertical pressure of the incumbent water on the triangular face of the dam, would be just equal to the lateral pressure in the direction of the stream. But as the base is more than twice the length, the vertical pressure exceeds the lateral; that is, the weight of the water helps to retain the dam in its place.

The excess of vertical pressure, and the bracing of the timbers supply a force to resist the momentum of the water in time of floods, and the blows of drift-wood, ice, and other floating bodies that may strike against the dam.

Tightness is secured by the piling and the facing plank. These swell and form a very compact and dense surface.—Sometimes the inclined plane is covered with soil to increase the ability of the dam to retain the water.

These wooden dams often last 10 or 12 years, as the timbers do not rot readily when under water.

When the stream is subject to high floods and to violent blows from drift-wood or ice, a stone dam is constructed.—This is built essentially on the same plan as the wooden ones; the triangular space below the facing being filled with stone, to give increased stability to the structure. The size and shape, the piling and facing remain the same. Sometimes the rocks are not put in every part of the dam, but in large pens at intervals across the stream. In all cases, but little dependence is to be placed on the bracing of the timbers or the workmanlike masonry of the wall, since the weight of the rock and the downward pressure of the water must give firmness to the mass, while the wooden facing and piling, with dirt resting on them, must retain the water.

If the bottom of the stream is of such material that it may be washed away by the water running over the dam, the lower side is inclined more or less, to break the force of the falling water and prevent its undermining the lower sills or walls.

187. *When the stream is wide, or the fall very rapid, it is better to make a canal at the side, than to build a dam across the stream.*

On the Ohio, around the falls at Louisville, a canal is used instead of dams. On the Schuylkill, sometimes one and sometimes the other plan is adopted.

188. *This improvement of rivers by slack-water navigation is expensive, and very seldom pays interest on the outlay.*

Over 1000 miles have been improved in this way in the United States; but several of these have been abandoned; the greater part have returned but small dividends to their stockholders, while a very few have been profitable.

The first cost for locks and dams is large; the ordinary repairs demand considerable money; while the extraordinary damages by floods and ice, are often so great as to require an expenditure but little less than the original outlay. In 10 or 12 years the wood work is entirely decayed, and must be replaced by new materials. Thus it happens that the demand for repairs and depreciation leaves little or perhaps nothing for dividends to the stockholders.

LECTURE XVI.

CANALS.

189. *Canals were used for commercial purposes by the ancients in Egypt, Persia, Italy, and China; and in the middle ages more or less by every country in Europe.*

In the earliest ages of the world canals were made, as they now are in many countries, to aid agriculture by supplying the fields with water; but even before the period of authentic history, the Isthmus of Suez was crossed by a canal so as to unite the Mediterranean and the Red Sea. Alexander opened canals in Persia, that had been dug before his invasion. The Romans constructed many in Italy, especially along the Po; and before the Christian era, the Chinese had connected Pekin, with the provinces of the empire, so as to transport by water a supply of rice and other grain for the large population of their capital.

In Italy, France, Holland and Germany, a large extent of artificial water navigation was opened before the eighteeuth century.

190. *From* 1750 *to* 1850, *the progress of canals has been rapid; though recently, since the introduction of Railroads, it has been everywhere very much checked.*

From 1755, when the Bridgewater canal was begun in England by Telford, to 1830 when railroads were successfully introduced, more than 3000 miles were constructed in Great Britain.

The immense transportation of coal, iron, and manufactured goods, has made these canals, for the most part, very profitable. Some have paid 100 per cent, per annum on their cost, and their stock has been 800 per cent above par.

In the United States, they were introduced before the Revolution, but the first work of importance was the Erie canal, in New York, from Albany to Buffalo, begun in 1817, and completed in 1825. This was 362 miles long, and cost about seven millions of dollars. This main line was connected with Lake Ontario and Champlain, and some other small lakes, by branches which cost about seven millions more. Large amounts have been expended recently in widening and deepening the Erie canal, and in enlarging its locks, until the whole outlay has now exceeded thirty millions, while the enlargement is not yet completed. The annual net income on all these works has been larger than the interest on their cost; so that, although the branches have been unprofitable, the State has gained by the expenditure, regarding her merely as a stockholder. The other advantages to the State and the city of New York have been immense. The whole amount of canals constructed in New York has been about 800 miles.

Canals have been built in Pennsylvania, along nearly all of her rivers, so that the whole amount in operation is about 1000 miles. Most of these were built between 1830 and 1840. Their cost has been about 30 millions, and but few of them have been profitable.

In Ohio there are 800 miles which have cost about 18 millions. They were begun in 1825; but most of them were completed between 1830 and 1840. The principal routes have been from Cincinnati to the Maumee river, and from Portsmouth on the Ohio to Cleveland on Lake Erie. These have not paid full interest on their cost, but have been very beneficial to the people of the State.

The Wabash Canal in Indiana connecting Lake Erie and the Ohio river, by the vallies of the Maumee and Wabash rivers, is a large and important work not yet completed; but it will soon be opened the whole way through.

The number of miles in all the States is over 4000, at a cost of 120 millions. A few of these have been abandoned; one-third of all have paid good dividends; the rest, though making but small returns on the capital invested in them, have conferred great advantages on the country.

Their recent progress has been very slow, as they cannot

compete with Railroads for passengers and light freight; and the principal routes, where a large amount of heavy freight is offered for transportation, are already occupied by canals.

191. *A canal is an artificial channel of water, from 30 to 50 feet wide, 4 or 5 feet deep, and so nearly level that the water has but a very slight movement.*

When the canal is narrow and shallow, and the locks small, the largest boats can be drawn by a single horse. For two-horse boats, a depth of 4 feet, and a width of 40 at the top, and locks 90 feet long, are sufficient; since on these, boats 12 feet wide and 90 feet long may be used. The cross section of the water displaced by these boats might have an area of about 36 feet, and this multiplied by 80, the average length, would give 2880 solid feet as the amount of water displaced. The weight of the boat is therefore $2880 \times 62\frac{1}{2}$ or 180000 lbs. The resistance on this is $180000 \div 720$ or 250 lbs., the proper load for two horses.

By making the canal wider and deeper, and the locks larger, the resistance is lessened, larger boats can be used, and the cost of attendance per ton is decreased, and the transportation can be effected with greater economy. On the Schuylkill, the Delaware and Hudson, and the Erie, large sums have been expended to advantage in enlarging these canals.

If water could be introduced between each set of locks, to supply the waste from evaporation and leakage, and the demand for the locks, there need be no current in the canal, and each basin would be perfectly level. But it is difficult to get such a supply of water without failure, and also without injury. It is usual therefore, to introduce the water at distances of 15 or 20 miles. Sometimes these intervals are as long as 40 or 50 miles, but this requires too much of a current.

A fall of 2 or 3 inches per mile is enough for the short intervals, and 5 or 6 inches for the longer.

192. *When water is very scarce, the boats are sometimes ransferred from one level to the other by an inclined plane.*

In China, locks are not used, and the boats are dragged up an inclined plane by the strength of men. But an overshot water-wheel is sometimes employed in Europe and in America for this purpose. To raise a boat of 100 tons by a lock of 8 feet lift, requires $90 \times 12 \times 8 \times 62\frac{1}{2} \div 2000$ or 270 tons of water. To raise the same boat by an ovreshot wheel would require only 150 tons, one-third of the full efficiency of the water being lost by this kind of wheel. The saving of water is therefore considerable.

The boats are raised by floating them on a car with wheels, and the car is drawn up on the inclined plane by a rope which is wound around a drum turned by the water wheel.

This method is not so simple as when locks are used; it is more costly at first, requires more for repairs, causes delays and accidents, and is therefore never used except when the scarcity of water renders it indispensable.

193. *The canal is usually made tight enough by the natural soil; but sometimes the bottom and sides are planked, or covered with hydraulic cement.*

If the soil is of clay, the bottom and sides of the canal are well rammed before introducing the water. If of sand, they are covered with a layer of clay. This does not make the surface water-tight, but the percolation is small and decreases after the first year, by the ordinary deposit from the water. If the base is rocky, and the planes of stratification come to the surface, it will be necessary to use plank or water cement to close these openings; and if cement is used, this must be itself covered two or three feet deep with earth to prevent injury from the shocks and the rubbing of the boats.

When there is an embankment, the walls are made very thick to lessen the waste of water. Not less than 8 feet at the water surface, when the soil is very compact; and usually 10 or 12. This wall is still thicker at the bottom, as the slope on either side is not less than $1\frac{1}{2}$ base to 1 in perpendicular height.

194. *The tow-path for the horses should be 10 or 12 feet wide, about 2 feet above the water surface, very nearly level, but inclining slightly outward.*

This width is necessary to permit the horses to pass easily; the height, to keep the path above the wave caused by the boat; the level grade, to save the horse the labor of lifting his body up hill; and the inclination, to give the horse a good foothold, and to prevent the rain-water from running into the canal.

175. *The rope by which the horse draws the boat is fastened to the middle of the boat and is not less than* 150 *feet long.*

If the rope is shorter than this, more of the horse's force is wasted in drawing the boat towards the bank. If the rope is 150 feet long, and the boat 15 feet from the path on which the horse walks, the force of the horse resolved in the direction in which the boat is moving is diminished only $\frac{1}{200}$ of his full effect.

176. *A supply of water is obtained from creeks along the route, from feeders, or reservoirs.*

When the canal crosses a stream which can be introduced into the canal, only a limited amount of water is admitted, for the whole might form too much of a current in the canal. In whatever way this limiting is effected, an excess will at times be introduced; and this must be permitted to run off by a waste-way at the side of the canal, made of rock, so as not to be washed away by the water escaping from the canal.

But few of the streams that are crossed are introduced into the canal, as it is difficult to prevent them from injuring it in times of freshets; most of them are passed either by a culvert when they are small, or by an aqueduct when large.

When the route does not meet a stream high enough to be introduced into the canal, a supply is sometimes obtained from distant streams by what is called a feeder. These are sometimes 10 or 15 miles long, and involve great expense.

When a sufficient supply of water cannot be obtained from streams or feeders, large reservoirs are sometimes constructed to collect the rain-water of winter for use in the summer.—However large these may be, they can never be depended on themselves, but are only an aid to streams that fail in the dry seasons of the year.

When all these sources fail, a steam engine has been occasionally used to raise a supply of water. This has been done on the Thames, and on the Union canal in Pennsylvania.—But as the demand for water for evaporation, for leakage, and for passing the boats through the locks, is large, this method is expensive and can seldom be used advantageously.

197. *The usual velocity for loaded boats is between* 2 *and* 2½ *miles per hour* ; *for passengers,* 3½ *to* 4.

The slower the velocity, the less is the resistance and the greater the useful effect of the horse; but below 2 or 2½ miles a horse cannot exert his force continuously. At higher velocities the resistance increases so rapidly, that even for passengers five miles per hour would be a wasteful expenditure of power. Besides, at this rate, the wave caused by the boat washes the sides of the canal and injures them so much that this velocity is absolutely prohibited.

198. *Steam can seldom be used to advantage on canals—only when they are very wide and deep.*

As high velocities cause great resistance and injure the sides of the canal, even with the submerged paddles or the screw, the steamboat must move slowly. Then its load or the number of boats it can draw becomes large, and the delay of passing through the locks wastes much time and steam. Hence the boats and canal and locks have to be very large to use steam advantageously. On the Erie canal horses only are used. On the broad and deep route between Philadelphia and New York the steam-tug is employed.

199. *The cost of a canal of the usual size,* 40 *feet wide at the bottom,* 50 *at the top, and* 5 *feet deep, with locks* 12 *feet long and* 100 *feet wide, is about* $20000 *per mile.*

This was the first cost of the New York and Ohio canals. If the rock-cutting is large, or the aqueducts numerous, or the walling or planking expensive; or if the canal is wider and deeper, and the locks larger than common, the cost may be much increased.

200. *The business that may be done on a canal is much larger than on a Railroad.*

As a load of 100 tons on a canal will only occupy 100 feet,

and as the boats can readily pass one another, the capacity of the canal would seem to be immense. But the delay at the locks imposes a limit to the number of boats. Not less than six minutes is required for filling a lock for a 100 ton boat, or twelve minutes for filling and emptying. This would allow five in an hour, or sixty in a day, or 6000 tons in one direction. But while the lock is emptying for an ascending boat, it may sometimes let down a descending one; or while filling for a descending boat, it may raise an ascending one. Thus 8 or 10000 tons may pass in 12 hours. By using the locks after night, still more may be passed. This, however, exceeds the capacity of a common railroad, even with a double track.

201. *On account of the large capacity of a canal, and the slight resistance in water, the charges for transportation are lower than on a railroad.*

Besides the cost of the motive force, tolls have to be paid to repair the canal and to return interest on the first cost. As the tonuage on which these are levied is large, the amount per ton is small. For both reasons therefore, the cost of transportation is less on canals than it is on railroads.

LECTURE XVII.

COMPARISON BETWEEN ROADS AND CANALS.

212. *When a country is new and unproductive, common roads are the only ones that are made.*

The amount of freight and travel being small, they will not pay for a more expensive road. As the country becomes more thickly settled, and its productions, whether of agriculture or manufactures, increase, the importance of good roads is felt; and if the character of the soil is such that the roads are much cut up and injured after rains or frosts, or if they are very sandy or marshy, a turnpike or a plank road may be desirable. When the freight or travel becomes still larger, railroads or canals may be constructed.

203. *If 25000 tons or 50000 passengers per annum pass over a route, a railroad may be substituted for a common road.*

As the cost of carriage on the common road is from 12 to $20 per ton per 100 miles, if the charge on the railroad is reduced to half this price, common wagons will be driven from the route, and freight and travel will be attracted for some distance off the line. If the charge averages $8 per ton, the receipts will reach $200000 for 100 miles. The expenses are, for transportation 25000 X $1.35, or $33750; for repairs of the track $500 per mile, or $50000. The net receipts will therefore be $116250, or about 6½ per cent. on a cost of $1,800000.

The receipts for 50000 passengers, at 4 cents per mile, would amount also to $200000. The expenses would be about the same as for the 25000 tons, counting the cost for two passengers and their baggage the same as a ton, because of the high velocity, the small net load, and the expensive cars.

204. *A Railroad may be built in the South to more advantage than any other artificial road.*

With turnpikes no comparison need be made; but with plank roads, this proposition is not so evident.

If the country is level and sandy, a plank road may be built cheaply and to great advantage to the horses and the travellers. Suppose the country so thickly settled that ten passengers on an average pass in both directions every day in the year, either in buggies or stages or carriages, and 60 loaded horses with freight.

When a plank road is built, suppose the passengers to double and the freight to double. The passengers will then number 20 per day, with about 10 horses; and the freight will not require more than 80 horses, because the efficiency of the horse is also doubled. The toll per day would then be, at two cents per mile for the first horses and one cent for the others, for a distance of 20 miles, 4+16 or $20. For 313 days this would give $6260. From this deduct $450 for three toll collectors, and $1000 for annual repairs of the road; and the net receipts will be $4810. If the planks be only 2 inches thick and the two sills 4 by 12, the cost of the planks at $7 per thousand will be for the 20 miles 20X7 (8X2+4×2) 5280 ÷ 1000 or $17741. For grading, ditching, and bridging, $200 per mile; for laying down the plank, and for toll houses $200 more; making for the 20 miles $8000 more, or $25741. Hence, if the road should last only five years, which is a fair limit for our warm climate, the annual receipts ($4810) will not even return the capital ($25741) to the stockholders, much less pay them a dividend.

In this estimate, the amount of planks, and the cost of grading are put down very low; and the tolls are as high as could be demanded. If they were raised to 1½ or 2 cents per mile per horse, the receipts would not probably be increased at all, since at this rate many of the wagons would prefer the common road.

If a railroad were built between the same points, the passengers will be increased to thirty or more per day. The freight will also be increased largely, but we will put it at what would be drawn by the 80 horses on the plank road, or 60 tons. The receipts from the passengers at 5 cents per mile, and for the freight at $1.60 per ton will be 30+96 or $126 per day. For the year this will give $126×313 or $40698. The cost of transportation will be (15+60)X313 X$1.35÷ 5 or $6338. The repairs at $500 per mile would be $10000; leaving net receipts $24360. The cost of the road over this favorable route may be put at $16000 per mile, or $320000; so that a dividend of nearly eight per cent, could be paid to the stockholders.

In this estimate nothing is allowed for depreciation, because $1.35, the cost of transportation per ton for a hundred miles, includes the repairs and depreciation of the cars and locomotives; and the $500 per mile for repairs will keep the superstructure and the iron in as good condition as when first laid down. The shortness of the line and the small amount of freight will not prevent the cheap working of the road, because a single locomotive can make two double trips or 80 miles per day, carrying both passengers and freight.

Thus it appears that while no dividend is received by the stockholders on the plank road, a railroad between the same points will give a handsome return.

205. *If the navigation of a river is interrupted much of the year, a railroad may be built advantageously along its banks ; but not otherwise.*

The Central Railroad has entirely driven the steamboats off the Oakmulgee. The South Carolina Railroad carries a large portion of the cotton from Augusta; and another railroad is building along the Savannah to compete with its boats. Along the Delaware and Hudson, where ice interrupts the navigation much of the year, railroads have been built which are used advantageously in the winter. But neither on these rivers, nor on the Ohio or Mississippi, can railroads compete successfully with steamboats for travel or freight, when the navigation is unobstructed. Passengers can be carried profitably on a boat at less than a cent a mile, and this amount will only pay the expenses on a railroad, especially at high velocities, and leave nothing for dividends to the stockholders. The whole cost of transporting passengers on the Georgia Railroad is about $1.35 for 100 miles, and this is as low as the average of other roads. On the Hudson river road, the level grades and the well built track tend to lessen the expense, but the large amount needed for repairs of cars and maintainance of way, at their high velocities, balance this in part; and there is reason to believe that the actual cost can not be reduced as low as on the river. The stock would thus be valueless, were it not that local freight, the mail, and the winter travel afford them some profitable business.

206. *For light freight and travel, railroads are preferable to canals. For heavy freight the canal is best.*

For ordinary travelers whose time is valuable, the railroad is best, on account of the rapidity of locomotion. But when time is not important, canals are best, because they are cheapest.

Formerly the Erie canal carried a large number of travelers; but since a railroad has been built along the same route, the canal is almost deserted. Even the emigrant passengers, who wish to travel very cheaply, for the most part prefer the railroad. But between Liverpool and Manchester far more pass by water than by railroad. The poor laborers, having but little money to spare for traveling, prefer the cheapest route.

For light freight the same reasons apply. The saving of interest with the rapid trains, and the regularity of the transit, secure the costly freight to the railroad, although the canal might carry it the cheapest. For coal which is worth 3 or $4 per ton, or for iron which may be worth $50, the canal is to be preferred.

Thus between Philadelphia and New York the freight carried on the canal far exceeds that by the railroads; not only coal, but a large amount of merchandise being transported on the canal. The whole tonnage, of all kinds, on the Liverpool and Manchester road is about 500000 tons, while one of the water routes between the same points has more than twice this amount. On the New York canal the tonnage exceeds two millions, although between Lake Erie and the Hudson, two railroad routes have by competition reduced the charges for transportation to the lowest possible limit.

The great Reading Railroad between Philadelphia and Pottsville, and the Schuylkill canal on the same route, seem at first sight to be exceptions to the general rule. Here the freight is almost entirely coal, which is commonly worth less than $4 per ton; yet the transportation on the railroad has reached 1,600000 tons, while on the canal the greatest amount has been 800000 tons.

But this road has been built with a very favorable grade for the down freight. For the whole distance from the mines to the Delaware, the road is either level or descending. The load for a locomotive is therefore much larger than on a common railroad. They work the whole year on the railroad; while the canal is interrupted 4 or 5 months by ice. The mines are beyond the termini of both lines, and the coal is brought by railroads to Pottsville, so that it must be unloaded before it can be started on the canal; and this involves not only expense but a loss of coal by breakage in the unloading. The transfer of the coal to the ships at Philadelphia is less costly from the Railraod, since the terminus is above the decks of the vessels and the load can be thrown into the hold without any labor. The distribution of the coal among the consumers in Philadelphia is cheaper from the railroad, since it can be carried to the centre of the city before it is unloaded. Yet with all these advantages, the tonnage on the canal has been gaining on the railroad, and will probably, before a long time, be equal to its full capacity.

The cost of transportation on a canal and a railroad was stated before at 50 cents, and $1.35 per ton per hundred miles; and besides this, a charge must be made for a dividend for the stockholders. But before a railroad can compete with a canal, this cost must be much reduced.

The several items that enter into this cost are for repairs of road, for repairs of cars, for motive power, for wages of persons employed in conducting the transportation, and for a dividend to the stockholders on the cost of the road.

The first two of these items cannot well be diminished on the best constructed road. If the loads are heavier and more numerous, the iron is worn away more rapidly, the wooden superstructure displaced, and the bridges injured.—The cars have to be increased just as rapidly as the loads, so that in these there can be no saving at all. Not so with the motive power. By making the road level a locomotive can draw a larger load without extra cost. Its wear and tear, its fuel, its engineer and fireman remain the same. The persons employed at the water-stations and depots are not increased, but the break-men and conductors and laborers are more numerous. The charge per ton for dividends to the stockholders diminishes rapidly as the business increases.

On the Reading Railroad they have reduced the cost of transportation from $1.35 to 60 cents, while 90 cents more is sufficient for a dividend to the stockholders, so that the whole charge is $1.50 per ton.

On a canal but little can be saved by increasing the business, or enlarging the locks and water-way. With a large broad and deep boat, the resistance for each ton and the cost of attendance are but slightly lessened. The return to the stockholders for each ton decreases of course as rapidly as the business increases. But the depreciation of the boats and the cost of loading and unloading remain the same. The boats have no return load and the cost of carrying them back is considerable, since the horses cannot move rapidly even with an empty boat.

On the Schuylkill canal they have not been able, for these reasons, to reduce the cost of transportation below 50 cents per ton, while 80 cents is necessary for a proper dividend to the stockholders, so that the whole charge is $1.30 per ton. As the business on the canal increases, this may hereafter be reduced.

Thus even on this superior road, with all its advantages, heavy freight cannot be transported as cheaply as on the canal.

207. *When a large amount of freight is passing between two places, a canal and railroad should both be built.*

A proper division of freight and travel is readily made by the wants and interests of the public who patronise the lines; while competition between the two reduces the cost and the charges as low as possible. Thus, between the Chesapeake and the Delaware, the Delaware and the Hudson, the Hudson and Lake Erie, Lake Erie and the Ohio, and Lake Michigan and the Mississippi, both railroads and canals are built, to the great advantage of the community.

LECTURE XVIII.

LEVELING.

208. *In constructing a Railroad or a Canal, great accuracy is necessary in the leveling.*

The channel of a canal is so straight and regular, that a very slight fall, only 4 or 5 inches in a mile, will give to the water a velocity of 1 mile per hour. An error, therefore, of a few inches might turn the water back towards its source, or give it too rapid a motion in the other direction, and thus make a current and perhaps exhaust the supply of water. On a railroad the same accuracy is not necessary. On neither is mathematical exactness wanted.

209. *Leveling is commonly done with a Spirit Level, attacked to a small Telescope, and supported by a* Tripod ; *besides which, is wanted a graduated rod.*

The rod being placed successively at two stations 100 feet apart, the telescope is directed to it, and the height of the line, where the horizontal wire of the telescope strikes the rod, above the ground is observed and recorded. The height on the first rod is called a *back-height,* and on the second, a *fore-height ;* and the excess of the back-height over the fore-height, gives the rise in the ground between these stations. In like manner the rise of the third over the second, and of the fourth over the third &c., are obtained. The sum of the first two gives the height of the third above the first ; this sum added to the third rise, gives the height of the fourth above the first. And so the height of each station above the first is found. If the fore-height should be more than the back-height, the difference should be regarded as negative ; and the additions, for the elevation of each station above the first, performed according to the rules of Algebra.

210. *When the rod is more than 200 feet from the leveling instrument, the distances of the first and last station from the instrument should be nearly equal.*

The true level being a curve, and the axis of the telescope, or the line along which the eye looks from the instrument to the rod, being a tangent to this curve, the back-heights and fore-heights will always be too large, by the space between the tangent and the curve. This space will be equal for the two observations, if the distances of the rod from the instrument should be the same. The errors in the back-heights and fore-heights being equal, will disappear in the subtraction, when the difference between them is taken to obtain the rise.

If the distances are small, the errors though unequal, are inappreciable. For one mile, the space between the tangent and a curve is two-thirds of a foot, and varies as the square of the distance. For 200 feet or $\frac{1}{26}$ of a mile, the space is $\frac{2}{3}\times(\frac{1}{26})^2$ or about $\frac{1}{1000}$ of a foot; which is the smallest amount that can be observed on the graduated rod.

Hence, when the distances of the rod are 200 feet or less, they need not be equal; if they are 4 or 500 feet they should be nearly equal; if they are much larger they should be made very nearly equal.

211. *Several observations are often made without moving the instrument, and then all but the first and last are both fore-heights and back-heights.*

This is done to save time in moving and adjusting the instrument. The second observation compared with the first shows the rise of the second station; and the third compared with the second observation shows the rise of the third station over the second; so that the second is twice considered; once, to be subtracted from the first, and again to have the third subtracted from it; and this is the same as to regard it first as a fore-height and then as a back-height.

When several observations are thus taken at once, the distances that should be kept equal, are the first and last; as any errors in the intermediate heights will not affect the last elevation.

212. *As a check against errors in the calculations, it is usual to find the rise of several stations by subtracting the sum of their fore-heights from the sum of their back-heights; this remainder being added to the height of the first of these stations will give the height of the last.*

As this is taking the difference of the sums, and the other method was to take the sum of the differences, the results must be the same.

213. *When several observations are taken without moving the instrument, the rise of the last of these over the first, can be found by comparing the first and last heights; this, added to the height of the first of these stations, will give the height of the last.*

Errors of addition and subtraction being easily made, these and other methods of checking the results are important in practice.

214. *In running a long line of levels, it is usual to take, every mile or two, the elevation of a cut made in a tree, or of some fixed permanent mark, to be starting points in subsequent levelings. These are called bench-marks.*

As the stakes driven down at each station may easily be displaced, the necessity of this is apparent, since the line must be often leveled before the work is completed.

215. *The profile of the line may be made from the heights of each station above the first; the heights being exaggerated* 10 *or* 20 *times or more, to make the rise and fall more apparent to the eye.*

If a horizontal line is drawn across the paper to represent the level of the first station; and by means of a scale with divisions close to the edge, the distances between each station are laid down along this line; and at each station the scale is held perpendicular to the horizontal line by applying its end to that line, and the heights then marked off, exaggerating each in the same ratio; a waving line drawn through the ends of these perpendiculars will represent the side view of the ground that has been levelled.

216. *The grade line for a rail-road is made by drawing it*

across the plot so that the cuttings above it shall be equal to the fillings below it—both being near each other.

This is usually done by the eye; but if greater accuracy is wanted, the cuttings and fillings may be calculated and thus made equal. If they are within a hundred yards of each other, they are said to be near; but it is better to carry the dirt, from the cuttings to a filling, 3 or 400 yards, than to obtain it from the side of the road.

The height of the grade line at each station is obtained by measuring it at its extreme points and noting the rise for the whole distance, and then, by proportion, finding the rise for each station, and then its height at each station.

217. *The cutting or filling at each station will be the difference of the heights of the ground and of the grade line.*

If, for example, the ground is 113.4 feet above the base line of the first station, and the grade 116.2 above, the ground will be 2.8 feet below the grade, and an embankment of this amount must be made. This is marked 2.8 B. When the ground is above the grade, the difference is marked A. So that A and B indicate the cuttings and fillings.

The following table will illustrate the several particulars referred to. At station 161, the back-height and fore-height were 4.817 and 2.581. The latter being the larger, the difference is positive and the ground rises. The instrument is not moved until the rod is carried to station 164, so that the fore-height of 161 is to be entered as the back-height of 162 and also of 163 and 164. The level of 160, or its height above the first station, is 65.532 and adding this to 2.236 gives 67.768 the level of 161. Adding this, algebraically, to the next difference, gives the level of 162. And so the rest are found. The level of 164 may be checked by taking 2.438 from 4.817 and adding the difference 2.379 to the level of 160, to get that of 164. So also 169 and 174 may be checked. The sum of all the back heights is 89.156 and of the fore-heights 85.647. The difference 3.509 being added to 65.532, gives 69.041, and is a check for 175. The heights of the grade line at 160 and at 170 being found to be 65.5 and 68.5, the difference, divided by 10, gives .3 as the rise for each station. This being added to 65.5, gives 65.8 as the grade for 161. The difference between the level and the grade of 161 or 2.0, is to be marked A, because the ground is above the grade.

Stations	Distances	Backheights	Foreheights	Differences	Levels	Grades	A & B
					65.532	65.5	0.0
161	100	4.817	2.581	2.236+	67.768	65.8	2.0 A
162			4.876	2.295—	65.473	66 1	.6 B
163			6.341	1.465—	64.008	66.4	2.4 B
164			2.438	3.903+	67.911	66.7	1.2 A
165		8.343	7.813	0.530+	68.441	67.0	1.4 A
166			6.716	1.097+	69.538	67.3	2.2 A
167			5.524	1.192+	70.730	67.6	3.1 A
	50		2.146	3.378+	74.108		
168			5.837	3.691—	70.417	67.9	2.5 A
169			8.914	3.077—	67.340	68.2	.9 B
170		5.334	9.642	4.308—	63.032	68.5	5.5 B
171			9.818	0.176—	62.856	68.8	5.9 B
172			2.519	7.299+	70.155	69.1	1.1 A
173			2.487	0.032+	70.187	69.4	.8 A
174			1.811	0.676+	70.863	69.7	1.2 A
175		4.362	6.184	1.822—	69.041	70.0	1.0 B
Totals		89.156	85.647	3.509+			

218. *The "distances out" of the side stakes from th centre depend on the cross slope of the ground, on the slope to be given to the sides, on the depth of the cut or the height of the bank, and on the width of the road-way.*

For a single-track rail-road, the width of an embankment should be 16 feet, and of a cut 24 feet, to leave a space beyond the track for the cars to run on, if they should get off the track, and to lessen the chance of the rails being disturbed by a slip of the bank, and to provide for ditches on each side at the excavations.

The depth of the cut or the height of the bank, is known in each case, from the grade table.

The side slope that ought to be given, depends on the

stiffness of the soil. If a cut is made in hard clay, the base of the bank may be to the perpendicular height as ¾ to 1; if an embankment is of stiff clay, it is 1 to 1; if sand is mixed with the clay, the slope is 1¼ or 1½ to 1; and if the soil is of sand, the slope is 2 to 1. Thus, fig. 21, if the bank is of sand BC : AB :: 2 : 1 or $\frac{BC}{AB}$ is 2. The quotient of BC÷AB is called the slope, and always represents the base when the perpendicular height is unity.

If the line of the ground across the road is level, the cross slope is nothing. But this seldom happens, and the cross slope must always be measured carefully with the levelling instrument, else the cubic yards removed by the workmen can not be accurately calculated.

When these four things are known, the distances out may be easily calculated.

Thus first, fig. 21, suppose the ground HC is level; the height of the bank LM to be d; the half breadth FL or LA to be b; and the slope $\frac{BC}{AB}$ to be r; then the distance out or MC is $b+dr$.

If b is 8 feet, d 4.8, and r 1½ to 1, the distance out, or MC, is 15.2. MH on the other side is the same.

If the figure be supposed to be turned upside down, it will represent a cut, instead of a bank; and the distances out can be calculated in the same way.

When there is a cross slope, that is, when the line NR is not level, the levelling instrument is commonly used to fix the side stakes at N and R. On one side, when the ground falls off, the distance out, which is now MS, being measured horizontally, is greater by CS than the MC obtained before; this CS=RS$\times r$ or sr, if we call s the difference of the heights of M and R. Hence, the practice is to observe the rod first at M, then move it out to R, until the difference s multiplied by r and then added to MC, should be equal to the measured length of MS; that is, $b+dr+sr$ must equal MS. On the other side, MP the distance out to N, is less than MH by HP, or NP$\times r$, or sr; that is, the rod must be moved out from M to N until $b+dr-sr=$ the measured length of MP.

In both cases, the distance out is $b+dr\pm sr$ where s represents the difference of level between the middle and the side stakes.

219. *The height of one point above another may be obtained by the theodolite, when the distance is known.*

As the levelling instrument gives its results slowly, it is sometimes desirable to obtain elevations more rapidly—even though they only approximate to the truth. This may be done by measuring the angle of elevation and then the true height = the distance × tangent of the angle of elevation.

The tangent of 1^0 being .017455, or about $1\frac{3}{4}$ hundreths, and the tangent of small arcs increasing nearly as the arc itself, the elevation will = distance × degrees of elevation $\times 1\frac{3}{4} \div 100$, when the arc is not over 10 or 15°.

Thus, if the angle of elevation of a point, 1200 feet distant, was $3^0 25'$, its height would be $1200 \times 3\frac{25}{60} \times 1\frac{3}{4} \div 100$ cr 71.75 feet.

220. *The elevation of an object may be found by directing the telescope to it, and noticing where the line of sight strikes two leveling rods; then leveling the telescope and noticing where it strikes the two rods again.*

The difference between the two spaces intercepted on the two rods, between the level line and the ascending line, will be the rise of the ascending line for the distance between the two rods. Hence the proportion: As the distance between the two rods, is to the rise of the ascending line, so is the distance of the object, to its height.

Thus, fig. 22, M being the leveling instrument, O the object, MN the distance, AD and EL the two rods, BF or CG the distance between them, BC and FH the two intercepted spaces, and GH their difference; then, CG : GH :: MN : ON.

221. *If the distance is short, a level line may be made by the common ditchers' level.*

This is a triangle, ABC, fig. 23, made by two narrow boards AB and BC, and united by the cross bar DE, with a plummet G, suspended by a string BFG, from B. To mark the point F, so that the string will show when A and C are on the same level, rest the triangle on two blocks and no where the string cuts DE; then turn it round and rest C on A's block, and A on C's, and note again where the string cuts DE. If the two points thus noted are the same, the blocks are level. If not, raise or depress one, until the point marked by the string is the same before and after the reversal. Then mark F and the triangle is ready for use.

Other marks may be made on DE near F, indicating a rise or fall of 1 in 100, 2 in 100, &c.

Sometimes a narrow horizontal opening or slit is cut at H, and a larger hole at L, across which a string or wire is stretched, and so adjusted that when A and C are level, the eye at H, before reversal, and at L after it, may see the same distant object M, along the line HL.

To use the instrument for ditching, cut away the ground AC until the string BG shall indicate by the mark at F whether the ground is level or falls at the required rate.

To use the sights H and L to mark out a level line, make AC level, by means of the string BFG, and the eye at H will look along the level line HLM.

To find out how much one point, as M, is higher than another, as H, raise or depress A until HLM is a straight line, then the string BFG will indicate at F the rate at which HL rises; and if the distance HM is known, the height of M over H may easily be found.

LECTURE XIX.

SURVEYING.

222. *The common surveyor's compass is not suited for the operations of the Engineer, as it will not give the courses of his lines with sufficient exactness.*

The thread used for the sights is too large, the divisions on the circle are not sufficienly minute, and the needle is broad, unsteady, and subject to local attraction. To overcome the first difficulty, a telescope with its small wires is added; for the second, a vernier is attached, so as to read the angles to single minutes, and sometimes to 15″; and for the third, the needle is dispensed with entirely, and each line is then run by measuring the angle it makes with the preceding line. This requires two circles in immediate contact with each other, one fixed or movable by a screw, and the other movable with the telescope. This is the construction of the common Theodolite, omitting the arcs for elevations; and this instrument is sometimes used. But as the Engineer often wishes to run straight lines, and this would require, at every transfer of the instrument, the measuring of an arc of 180°, this is avoided by making the telescope revolve on a horizontal axis, and then its reversal will continue the straight line first run. The instrument is then called a transit, from its likeness to the Astronomical transit, which revolves like this in a vertical plane.

With the transit or Theodolite, a straight line is easily run. After beginning at the point A, as many stations are pointed out as can be seen, and then the instrument is transferred to the last one observed, and its centre placed carefully over the stake, by means of a plummet. The rod is now placed at A, and the telescope directed back towards it. If then the telescope of the transit is made to revolve so as to point in the opposite direction, or if the Theodolite is turned 180°, the former straight line will be continued.

223. *In using the transit, the several courses are indicated by deflections, by which is meant the angle made by a new course with the last produced.*

To change the course, for example, 3°, the operations would be, sight back to the last position of the transit, reverse, and deflect 3°. This is inserted on the record on the right or left side, according as the deflection is on the right or left of the preceding line. A compass is attached to the instrument, as a check against gross errors of observation, or of record, or of calculation. The course of the first line being observed by the compass, the courses of all the rest will be found by applying the several deflections, and can then be compared at any time with the needle, and gross errors detected.

224. *The surveyor, besides marking out the several stations, and recording and plotting the courses and distances, makes a sketch of the country he passes over.*

He draws a line up and down the middle of the page, and notes on that page the fences and streams that cross his line, and their courses and bendings, the rise and fall of the ground on either side, the direction and extent of the ravines or ridges or irregularities, and the situation of the several objects that are near him, such as the dwellings, the woods, and the fields, as far as all these can be copied by a practised eye. This sketch is transferred to his plot, which not only represents the line surveyed, but the several objects near that line, which it may be necessary to be acquainted with, in the subsequent location of the route.

225. *When a river, or marsh, or obstruction of any kind interrupts the survey, the distance across may be obtained in several ways, by the principles of Geometry and Mensuration.*

By measuring a base line and taking the angles at each end, the distance can easily be calculated by Trigonometry. But the logarithmic tables not being always at hand, recourse is often had to other methods in the field. The unknown distance is made the side of a parallellogram or of an isosceles triangle, and thus becomes known by its equality to other sides. Or it may be made the side of a right-angled-triangle, and then found by (47. 1.) Euclid. Or it may be found by similar triangles described on the ground:

1. If MN be a marsh, the distance AD across it, may be found by running AB any course and distance, then transferring the instrument to D, and running DC parallel to AB. Then, BC being measured, will be equal to AD.

2. Again. Make at A the angle DAE equal 45^0; measure AE, and make AEF equal 90^0; measure EF equal to AE; then F will be in the line AD, and $AF^2 = AE^2 + EF^2$.

3. Again. Make the angle DAG of any convenient size;

and GA of any length; set up three flags D, L, and F in the line; at G make the angle AGH equal half the supplement of GAH and fix the point H in the line GH and also in AD by means of the three flags D, L, and F. Then AH=AG.

These methods admit of several variations, so as to accommodate them to the different situations in which they may be wanted. Other methods may also be adopted, founded on similar principles.

226. *If a swamp intervenes, it is sometimes desired to return to the original line. This is done by running several lines, as AB BC CD and DE; then Ed* dc cb *and* ba, *each equal to the first, and making the same angles with the original line, but turned in the opposite direction.*

It is evident that as far as AB diverts the surveyor from the original line, just so far will *ab* bring him back; for they are equal, and make equal angles with the first line.

227. *The distance of any point from the line, may be found by taking its bearing from two known points.*

If these two points are in one straight line, its course being known, the angles and one side of a triangle will be given to find the other sides. If several courses and distances have been run between the two points where the observations are taken, the course and distance of the straight line joining them may be found by taking the Algebraic sum of all the northings and southings, and of the eastings and westings of all the intermediate lines as the departure and difference of latitude of the straight line between the two points; and hence its course and distance may be found, and then the course and distance of the given point.

LECTURE XX.

LOCATION OF A RAIL ROAD.

238. *The location of a road consists in laying out long lines instead of the short ones first surveyed, and uniting these long lines by a circle touching both.*

As the danger of running off the track is greater on the curves, and as the flange friction is very large and hard to be overcome, the curves should be few and with as large a radius as possible. None less than a thousand feet radius should be allowed; and it is very desirable to keep this limit as large as 2000 feet.

If two circles are introduced at a bend in the route, the two must touch one another, and each touch one of the straight lines. No sudden change of direction will thus be made in passing from the first straight line to the first curve, or from the first curve to the second, or from the second curve to the straight line.

239. *These circles are first marked out by running* 100 *feet chords; and when the rails are laid down, by shorter chords, as* 25 *feet or the length of the rail.*

It would not be possible to lay out these large circles by revolving a long radius round a centre, since it would be obstructed by intervening objects. The several 100 feet chords coincide very nearly with the arc; near enough for the earth-work to be done along them. With the smallest radius (1000 feet) the distance of the middle of the chord from the arc is only $50 \times 50 \div 2000$ or $1\frac{1}{4}$ feet. And for larger circles the interval is still less.

When, however, the superstructure is to be laid down, the ends of the rails are to be placed on the curve. The rail itself is seldom bent to coincide with the curve, since even when the radius is 1000 feet and the rail 18 feet long, the deflection of the middle would only be $9\times9\div2000$, or less than half an inch.

240. *The angle at the centre of the circle subtended by a 100 feet chord is called the curvature* (*c*); *the angle between a tangent and a 100 feet chord, the tangential angle* (*T*); *and the exterior angle made by the two tangents to the curve, the total deflection* ($2d$).

Let ABD and DCE (fig. 26) be two straight lines between which the curve B 1 2 3 4 5 C is to be located, having O its centre, and B1, 12, 23 &c. = 100 feet; the angle BO1 is the curvature (c), DB1 is the tangential angle (T), and FDE is the total deflection ($2d$).

The following propositions concerning these angles and this figure are easily proved:

1. The tangential angle T is equal to half the curvature c. For 1BO and $T=90^0$, because a tangent is at right angles to the radius; and 1BO and $\frac{1}{2}c=90^0$, because they are the two acute angles of the right angled triangle BOG. Hence $T=\frac{1}{2}c$.

2. The angles at the circumference subtended by a 100 feet chord are equal to T; because they are all equal to half of c. Thus $B31=\frac{1}{2}BO1=\frac{1}{2}c=T$.

3. If a long chord subtend n of the 100 feet chords, the angle it subtends at the centre is nc, and at the circumference nT. Thus $BO3=3c$ and B43 is 3T; BO5 is $5c$ and BC5 is 5T.

4. If a long chord be produced, the exterior angle made by it and the next 100 feet chord is $(n+1)$ T. Thus, if B4 be produced to L, the angle $L45=(n+1)T$. For (32.1.) $L45=B54+4B5=nT+T$. In like manner $H12=2T$.

5. The angle made by a long chord produced with a tangent is equal nT. Thus if 4M is a tangent at 4, $L4M=nT$; because $L45=nT+T$ and $M45=T$ (by definition of T); hence $L4M=nT$.

6. The number (n) of 100 feet chords between B and C $=2d+c$. For FDC=BOC, since each is the supplement of BDC; and $BOC=BO1+1O2+2O3+3O4$ &c. $=nBO1=nc$; that is $2d=nc$; or $n=2d\div c$.

7. The tangent BD$=100d\div c$, very nearly. For BD$=\frac{1}{2}$(BD+DC)$=\frac{1}{2}$ arc BSC nearly $=\frac{1}{2}$ (B1+12+23+34+45+5C)$=\frac{1}{2}\,100n=\frac{1}{2}(100\times 2d\div c)=100d\div c$.

8. The tangent BD is longer than $\frac{1}{2}$BSC; so that, it is more than $100d\div c$. It is more nearly $(100d+d^3\div 100)\div c$.

9. The radius of the circle is very nearly $5730\div c$. In the triangle BOG where BG$=50$, if we take BOG or $\frac{1}{2}c=30'$, 1°, $1\frac{1}{2}^\circ$, and 2°, we find BO by Trigonometry to be 5729.7, 2865.0, 1910.1 and 1432.7 or very nearly $5730\div 1$, 2, 3, 4 or c.

10. The deflection of the first chord B1 from BD is T; of the second 12 from B1 is 2T, or from BD it is 3T; of the third from 12 is 2T or from BD it is 5T &c., the deflection of every chord from the first tangent being 2T, except of the first chord which is T. Hence the deflection of the nth chord is $(2n-1)$T.

11. If the course of the tangent be known, the course of the nth chord will be found by adding or subtracting $(2n-1)$T to the course of the tangent.

12. The distance P1 from the curve at 1 to the tangent is $\frac{7}{4}$T or $\frac{7}{8}c$, and varies as the square of the arc or the chord. For it is equal to B1 sin.T. But B1 is 100, and sin. $1^\circ=.01745$, and sin.T$=.01745$T for small arcs, and 100 sin. T $=1.745$T or $\frac{7}{4}$T nearly. And as it is equal to the versed line of the arc, it varies as the square of the chord or of the arc.

241. *When the ground is suitable for any curve, select one with a very large radius*, 10 *or* 20000 *feet.*

The larger the radius, the less is the flange friction and also the danger of running off the track. To mark out the curve on the ground, we must know from the previous survey the total deflection or $2d$. As the radius is arbitrary and must be large, we may take $c=1^\circ$ or $30'$ or $12'$; for the radius would be in these cases $5730\div 1$ or $\frac{30}{60}$ or $\frac{12}{60}=5730$, 11460 and 28650. To find the point B where the curve begins, we must find BD. By (7) it$=100d\div c$ or by (8) $(100d+d^3\div 100)\div c$. To find the number of 100 feet chords from B to C, we have (by 6) $n=2d\div c$. As T$=\frac{1}{2}c$, every thing is known that is necessary to run the curve.

Example. Let FDC=$5^0.30'$, and let the ground be level or suitable for any curve.

Assume a curvature of 18′. That is, let BO1=18′ and BOG=9′. Then by Trigonometry we find BO=19098.6. In BOD we have the angle BOD=$\frac{1}{2}$ of $5^0.30'$ or $2^0.45'$. Hence by Trigonometry BD=917.37. The number of 100 feet chords from B to C is $5\frac{30}{60} \div \frac{18}{60}$ or $330 \div 18$ or 18.33. The tangential angle is $\frac{1}{2}c$ or 9′. And every thing is now known that is needed to run the curve.

This example has been solved accurately by Trigonometry. It could have been done more easily by the methods before explained. We assumed $c=18'$; hence $T=9'$; $n=2d \div c=5^0.30' \div 18'=18.33$; and BD=(by 7) $100d \div c=916.6$; or more accurately (by 8) $(100d+d^3 \div 100) \div c$ or $(275+20.8 \div 100) \div \frac{18}{60}$ or $275.208 \div \frac{3}{1}$ or 917.36.

The 916.5 is an approximate result obtained by supposing the tangent and the chords equal, and is sufficiently exact for most purposes. The 917.36 obtained by the formula agrees almost exactly with the Trigonometrical result and is as accurate as can be desired for practice.

These calculations being made, the curve may be run as follows: Measure from the angle D backwards 917.36 feet and B is found. Place the transit at B, sight along BD, deflect T or 9′ and the telescope points to 1; measure B1=100 feet and 1 is found. Deflect at B again the angle 1B2 or T or 9′ and the telescope points to 2; measure 12=100 feet, and 2 is found. Deflect again 9′ and measure 23=100 feet and 3 is found. And so also find 4. Suppose now that no farther distance can be observed from B. Transfer the transit to 4; sight back to B; reverse it, and the telescope points to L; deflect L45 or (by 4) $(n+1)$ T or 5T=45′, and the instrument points now to 5; measure 45=100 feet and 5 is obtained. Deflect at 4 the angle 546=T=9′ and measure 100 feet and 6 is found. So also mark out 7, 8, 9, 10, 11, and 12. If the ground beyond 12 can not be seen from 4 transfer to 12; sight back to 4; reverse and deflect (by 4) (8+1) T or 81′, and the telescope now points to 13; measure 100 feet and 13 is found. So also 14, 15,

16, 17 and 18 may be found. The number of chords to be run was 18.33. The fraction .33 will subtend at the instrument .33T or 3′. Deflect therefore 3′ and measure 33 feet, and the end of the curve C is reached. Transfer now to C; sight back to 12, the last position of the telescope: reverse and deflect now (by 5) nT, n representing the number of intervening chords; they are 6.33; deflect therefore 6.33T or 57′ and the instrument now points along the tangent CE, and the curve is completed.

The circle has now been run with three removals of the transit; being stationed at A, 4, 12, and C. It might have been done by moving it at every chord; then the deflection every time would have been 2T or 18′. It is better and more convenient to run several chords without removing the transit.

If in marking out the 8th chord, it should be desired to check its course with the compass; suppose the course of BD to be N 20°. 10′ W and that the curve is to the east of BD. The course of the eighth chord is now (by 10 and 11) 20°. 10′—15 T or 20°. 10′—135′ or N 17°.55′W

LECTURE XXI.

LOCATION CONTINUED.

242. *If the point where the curve should leave the tangent is given, find the curvature and the tangential angle; take for T a whole number, and find the point where this curve will leave the tangent.*

It seldom happens that the ground is suitable for any curve. There is usually some point where it is better that the curve should start off, so that a cutting or a filling may be lessened or a marsh or a rock avoided, or the track in some way improved. When that is the case, BD becomes known.

But (by 7) BD$=100d\div c$, and hence c is found, since d is known from the previous survey. Now T$=\frac{1}{2}c$; and the curvature and the tangential angle are thus determined.

As T will generally be a fraction, it would be troublesome to read it off on the transit, and it is usual, therefore, to alter T slightly on this account. This will change the size of the curve and make it leave the tangent at a different point from A. The change is, however, very slight, and the point where the curve leaves the tangent will seldom make any appreciable difference in the route.

Example. Let the total deflection, or $2d=6^0.20'$ & BD $=1200$ feet.

To solve this by Trigonometry, we have in BOD the side BD$=1200$ and BOD$=\frac{1}{2}(6^0.20'.)$ Hence BO$=21723$. Now in BOG we have also BG$=50$, and hence the angle BOG or $\frac{1}{2}c=7'.55''$. If we solve it (by 7) we have $1200=100d\div c$ or $c=3\frac{10}{60}\div 12$ or $190'\div 12$ or $15'.50''$, and T$=\frac{1}{2}c$ or $7'.55''$; the same as before. Take now T$=8'$, and mark out the curve. $c=2$ T or 16 D B. (by 8) is $(100d+d^3\div 100)\div c$ or $(100\times3\frac{1}{6}+31.75\div 100)\div\frac{16}{60}$ or $(19000+19.05)\div 16$ or 1188.7. And $n=3^0.10'\div 16'$ or 11.875. These elements are sufficient to run the curve. Measure from D 1188.7 to B; at B direct the telescope along BD and deflect 8′ and it points to 1; measure B1$=100$ feet and 1 is found. Deflect 8′ again and measure 100 feet from 1, and 2 is determined. In like manner, fix the stakes at 3, 4, and 5. At 5 suppose it is necessary to move the transit. Transfer it to 5, sight back to B, treverse, and deflect (by 4) $(n+1)$ T or 6T or 48′; measure now 100 feet and 6 is found; deflect 8 and measure another 100 feet a nd 7 is found. So mark out 8, 9, 10 and 11. After 11, a fractional chord .875 is to be run. Deflect .875T or 7′, measure 87.5 feet and the end of the curve or C is arrived at. Transfer now to C, sight back to the last position of the instrument at 5, reverse, and deflect (by 5) nT or 6.875T$=55'$ and the telescope will then be pointed along the tangent line CE.

To find a check for the course of the 5th chord, we have it (by 10)=course of BD$\mp(2n-1)$T=course of BD$\mp72'$.

243. *To run the circle at a given distance from the angular point where the two tangents meet, make the curvature or* $c=\frac{7}{8}d^2\div$ *this distance.*

For the distance from the curve to the tangent at 1 is (by 12)$=\frac{7}{4}$T or $\frac{7}{8}c$; and at the distance of n chords of 100 feet, it is $n^2 \times \frac{7}{8}c$. But the chords from B to S are $d\div c$. Therefore BS$=\frac{7}{8}cd\div c^2$ or $c=\frac{7}{8}d^2\div$ BS.

Example. Let FDE$=15^0.30'$ and DS$=30$ feet. Then $c=\frac{7}{8}(7\frac{3}{4})^2\div 30=1^0.45'$. T$=\frac{1}{2}c$ or $52\frac{1}{2}'$. The number of chords to be run is $2d\div c$ or $15^0.30'\div 1^0.45'$ or 8.857. The distance BD$=(100d+d^3\div 100)\div c$ or $779.65\div 1\frac{3}{4}$ or 445.5.

This solution is approximate. To make it exact, find from the tables, the versed sine of $\frac{1}{2}d$ and it will give DS when the radius is unity. Divide this DS into DS as known, and the quotient will give the radius. Then in BOG the angle BOG or $\frac{1}{2}c$ may be found.

Thus in the example above; versed sine of $7^0 45'$ is .0091341, divide into 30 and we have radius 3284.8. Hence in BOG we find BOG or $\frac{1}{2}c$ or T$=52'.20''$; nearly the same as before.

To mark out the curve, with T$=52\frac{1}{2}'$ measure BD or 445.5 feet from D and B is found. At B deflect T and measure 100 feet to 1. Deflect T again and the telescope points to 2. And so 3, 4, and 5 are staked off. Move now the instrument to 5, sight back to B, reverse, (by 7) deflect $(5\div 1)$ T or 315', and the instrument then points to 6. Deflect now T and 7 is found. In like manner find 8. Now for the fractional chord, deflect .857 T or 43' and measure 85.7 feet, and we arrive at the end of the curve or C. Transfer now to C, sight back to 5, deflect (by 8) 3.857T or $200\frac{1}{2}'$ and the telescope is then directed along the tangent CE.

244. *To run the curve through a given point R, whose distances from the tangent and the angular point RT TD, are known. Let the number of* 100 *feet in BT$=x$ and in TD$=a$. Then (by* 9) $d\div c=x\div a$, *and (by* 12). *TR* $=\frac{7}{8}x^2c$; *and hence c may be found.*

This when solved, gives a quadratic equation; but it will be best to solve it by trials, as T and c are not often wanted exact—only to the nearest whole number.

Example. Suppose $2d=16^{0}$ and $DT=550$ feet and $SR=20$, it is required to run the curve through or very near R.

Let $c=1^{0}$ and the first equation $d\div c=x+a$ becomes $8=x+5\frac{1}{2}$ or $x=2\frac{1}{2}$; and the second, $SR=\frac{7}{8}n^{2}c$ becomes $20=\frac{7}{8}\times 2\frac{1}{2}^{2}=5$. This second equation not being satisfied, c is not$=1^{0}$.

Let $c=45'$ or $\frac{3}{4}$ of 1^{0}; then we have $x+5\frac{1}{2}=8\div\frac{3}{4}$ or $x=5\frac{1}{6}$; and $20=\frac{7}{8}(5\frac{1}{6})^{2}\times\frac{3}{4}=17\frac{1}{2}$; so that the second equation is now very nearly satisfied.

Let now $c=43'$; then $x+5\frac{1}{2}=8\div\frac{43}{60}$ or $x=5.66$; and $20=\frac{7}{8}\times 5.66^{2}\times\frac{43}{60}=20.06$; so that both equations will be almost exactly satisfied if $c=43'$.

With this then run the curve. Find $BD=(100d+d^{3}\div 100)\div c=805.12\times\frac{60}{43}=1123.4$; and $T=21\frac{1}{2}'$; and $n=2d\div c$ or 22.325. Thus, we have the point where the curve starts, the tangential angle, the curvature, and the number of 100 feet chords that subtend the curve between the two tangents. Which comprise every thing necessary to mark out the curve on the ground.

245. *To alter a curve already run, so that the final tangent on the new curve shall be parallel to the final tangent on the first; find the distance between the last two tangents measured on a line parallel to the first tangent, and start the new curve at this distance on the first tangent from the original starting point.*

It may happen from wrong measurements of DB, or from other causes, that the curve BC runs too far and crosses the line UW which it ought to touch, or fails to meet it. If the course of UW and BD had been correctly measured, the tangent CE would be parallel to UW, but C might be inside or outside of UW.

If now we run CV parallel to DB and start the curve anew at A, making BA equal to CV, it is evident that the whole curve is removed towards A, so that it will now touch both AD and UW.

246. *To alter a part of a curve so that the final tangent on the new part shall be parallel to the former final tangent; return backwards* n *chords and run a new circle, such that its tangential angle* (T') *shall be to the former tangential angle* (T) *as* $\frac{7}{4}n^2 T$ *is to* $\frac{7}{4}n^2 T \pm$ *the perpendicular distance between the two tangents.*

It may happen that the first part of the curve as B123 has been already graded, or is in some way so fixed that it is desirable to retain it, while the rest of the curve crosses UW which it ought to touch, the tangent CE being parallel to UW.

It is now necessary to run a new curve 3U touching the curve B123 at 3 and touching also UW. Since the curves 3U and 3C have the same tangent at 3, and parallel tangents at U and at C, they contain the same number of degrees; hence their radii are as their versed sines. But their radii (by 3) being$=5730\div c$ and $5730\div c'$ vary inversely as c or as T. And the versed sine of C3 or the distance of 3 from the tangent CE is (by 11)$=\frac{7}{4}n^2$T, and the distance from the tangent UW$=\frac{7}{4}n^2$T$-b$, if we represent by b the perpendicular distance between CE and UW. Hence, $T' : T :: \frac{7}{4}n^2 T : \frac{7}{4}n^2 T - b$ which is the rule given above.

If the curve 3C had fallen inside of UW the distance b in the above proportion would have been positive instead of negative.

As the point 3 from which the new curve starts is any point, the new circle may be started from B and the whole curve run anew.

Example. Suppose the curve BC to have been run with a tangential angle (T) of 45′; that the total deflection $2d$ was 16°.30′; that the curve BC extended 20 feet beyond UW; and that the first three of the chords on BC were so fixed that it was desirable to retain them.

Here the tangential angle T being 45′, c is $1\frac{1}{2}$° and the number of chords from B to c is (by 6) 16°.30′ $\div 1\frac{1}{2}$° or 11.

Three of these being retained, the number from 3 to C or n is =8. And n^2 T is $64 \times \frac{3}{4}$ or 48. And n^2 T$-b$=48–20=28. Hence 28 : 48::45′ : T′=$77\frac{1}{7}$′.

It is necessary to run the curve with this fractional angle, if the point 3 and the tangent UW are fixed. If only 3 is fixed and it would be allowable to change UW slightly, T might be taken 77′.

The angle which the chord 34 on the first curve made with BD was (by 11) (8–1) T or 7T. The angle made by the tangent at 3 with BD was therefore 6T or 270′ or 4°.30′. Hence the angle between the tangent at 3 and CE is 16°.30′ –4°.30′ or 12°. The curvature c' for the new curve is 154′, and the number of chords or n' is 12°÷ 154′ or 4.675.

To mark out the curve. Set the transit at 3, sight back to B, reverse, deflect (by 5) 3T or 135′, and the telescope points along the tangent at 3. Deflect still farther 77′, and the telescope points to 4 on the new curve; measure 100 feet, and 4 is found. Deflect 77′ and measure 100 feet and 5 is found. In like manner 6 and 7 may be staked off. There yet remains a fractional chord of .675 to be run. Deflect now .675 T or 52′, and measure from 7 the chord 67.5 and the end of the curve or U is reached. Transfer now to U, sight back to 3, deflect 4.675 T or 360′ and the telescope points along the tangent UW.

247. *To mark out the arc for the rails, divide the product of the segments of the chord by the diameter, and the distance of the arc from the chord will be found.*

This rule is nearly right (Euc. 35. 3.) for the middle of the arc, where the perpendicular to the chord passes through the centre; but it is also sufficiently correct for the other points, since the perpendicular, produced to the other side of the circle, is very nearly equal to the diameter.

Example. Let the radius be 2000 feet and the rails 18 feet. The segments of the chord at the end of the first rail will then be 18 and 82, and the distance of the arc from the chord will therefore be 18×82 ÷4000 or .369 of a foot. For the end of the second rail, it will be 36×64÷ 4000 or .576. For its middle, it will be 27×73÷4000 or .493.

Stretch then a string from one station to another, and measure these distances from the string for the ends and other parts of the rails.

248. *To mark out the arc for the rails by the transit, place it on the curve, direct the telescope to the end of the chord, deflect* $mT \div 100$ *and the telescope will be directed to that point of the curve whose distance from the station is* m.

As the 100 feet chord subtends the angle T at the circumference, the chord m will subtend $m\,T \div 100$.

LECTURE XXII.

MENSURATION.

249. *Timber is bought by board measure, in which the unit is one foot square and one inch thick.*

If the thickness is less than an inch, it is common to count it an inch; but if it exceeds an inch, the additional thickness is charged for.

In measuring sills and scantling by this rule, the same price is paid for them as if they were sawed an inch thick. They are therefore better paid for than the inch plank.

250. *Masonry is measured by the perch of 25 solid feet; brick work by the thousand brick, no deduction being made for wood worked into the wall.*

A linear perch or rod is $16\frac{1}{2}$ feet; and if the wall is $1\frac{1}{2}$ feet thick, the solidity will be $24\frac{3}{4}$ feet. The unit used by the Engineer is a little more than this, 25 and not $24\frac{3}{4}$.

The number of bricks is estimated by multiplying together the length of all the rows, the thickness of the wall counted in bricks, and the number in a given row, and the product divided by the length of that row.

251. *Carpentry is measured by the hundred square feet, no deduction being made for doors, windows, &c.*

The length and breadth being multiplied together, and the product divided by 100 gives the number of squares; and the trouble of adjusting the ends of the plank at any break in the surface being considerable, the charge includes the cost of covering the opening.

252. *Plastering and painting are usually measured by the square yard, no deduction being made for windows, &c. some pieces of painting however are measured by the linear yard or foot, and some are paid for by the piece.*

Doors, windows, &c. are painted by the piece; a line of fencing by the linear length; the out side of a house by the square yard, or by the 100 square feet.

253. *The weight of materials is found by multiplying their solidity in feet by* $62\frac{1}{2}$, *and this by the specific gravity of the substance.*

As a cubic foot of water weighs $62\frac{1}{2}$ lbs., and the specific gravity shows how much heavier the material is than water, this product will evidently give the weight.

For rock, the specific gravity is commonly about $2\frac{1}{2}$; for green timber very nearly 1; for dry pine $\frac{1}{2}$; for dry oak .7; for cast iron 7.2; and for wrought iron 7.8.

Approximate rules founded on this are, that green wood weighs about 5 lbs. per foot of board measure; dry pine, about $2\frac{1}{2}$; and dry oak $3\frac{1}{2}$. Iron about $\frac{1}{4}$ of a lb. per cubic inch. About 13 feet of rock make a ton.

254. *The contents of a circle are* $\frac{3}{4}$ *of the square of the diameter; and of a sphere,* $\frac{1}{2}$ *of the cube of the diameter.*

The true amounts are a little larger than this; but these rules will often be near enough right.

255. *To find the bushels in any space, take* $\frac{8}{10}$ *of the solid feet contained in the space.*

The true size of a bushel being 2150.42, eight-tenths of this will be 1720.336, which is nearly the same as 1728 inches or a solid foot.

256. *To find the sine of a small arc, take* $\frac{1}{60}$ *of the number of degrees in the arc.*

As the sine of 30^0 is $\frac{1}{2}$ radius, the other small arcs as a first approximation may be taken proportional to this. The error in this rule will in no case exceed .05.

257. *To find the sine or tangent of small arcs, take* $\frac{7}{400}$ *of the degrees in the arc.*

Up to 15^0, this will never be wrong more than .005, for either sine or tangent.

258. *To find the sine and tangent more accurately, divide* 3.14159 *by* 180 *and it gives* .017453 *the length of one degree of arc; subtract from this* $\frac{8}{9}d^2\div$ *a million, for the sine, and add twice this for the tangent; multiply these results by the number of degrees in the arc.*

EXAMPLE. Let the arc be $8^0.30'$. The length of 1° is .017453; and $\frac{8}{9}\times 8\frac{1}{2}^2$ is 64; hence the sin. $8\frac{1}{2}°=(.017389)8\frac{1}{2}$ or .147807; and the tan. $8\frac{1}{2}°=(.017581)8\frac{1}{2}$ or .149439. The true values in the tables are .147809 and .149441. Up to 30°, the results will generally be correct to four decimals.

259. *To find the cosine, subtract versed sine from unity. The versed sine is* $3d^2\div 20000$, *representing the degrees by* d, *or more accurately it is* $.00015231d^2-\frac{1}{6}(.00015231d^2)^2$.

EXAMPLE. The versed sine of $8\frac{1}{2}°$ is $72\frac{1}{4}\times 3\div 20000$ or .0108375. Or more accurately; $.00015231\times 72\frac{1}{4}$ is .0110044 & $\frac{1}{6}(.0110)^2$ is .0000202 & hence versed sine of $8\frac{1}{2}$ is .0109842.

Versed sines are often wanted by the Engineer, and this rule gives very accurate results up to 30.

250. *Earth-work is measured by the cubic yard. If the solid is a prism, the product of the end area into the length will give the solidity.*

EXAMPLE. Let a rail-road cut be 10 feet deep and 100 feet long, the slope $1\frac{1}{2}$, and the breadth at the bottom 24 feet. Here the half breadth at the top is $12+10\times 1\frac{1}{2}$ or 27 feet. And the area of the trapezoidal end is (27+12)10 or 390 feet. And the solidity in yards is $390\times 100\div 27$ or 14444.

Algebraically, this solidity is $(2b+dr)dl\div 27$. For the distance out is $b+dr$. And the area of the trapezoid is $(b+b+dr)d$. And the product of this into the length (l) divided by 27 will give the solidity in yards.

If the depth of the two ends is not the same, take the average depth, and to the solidity thus found, add $\frac{1}{12}x^2rl$, representing by x the difference of the depths of the two ends.

If from the upper edge AB (fig. 27) of the less end, a horizontal plane ABGH be supposed to pass; and through A and B, two vertical planes AGL and BHM; the whole solid ADNE will be divided into a prism ADFG, a wedge ABHL, and two triangular pyramids AGLO and BHMN.

The solidity of the wedge, and the prism will be found correctly by taking the average depth of the two ends as an average prism. Not so for the pyramids.

The average gives for the two pyramids two triangular prisms whose ends are HPR and GST, where HP is $\frac{1}{2}x$ and PR is $\frac{1}{2}xr$. Hence HPR is $\frac{1}{8}x^2r$. And the solidity of the two prisms is $\frac{1}{4}x^2rl$. The end area HMN of the pyramid is $\frac{1}{2}x \times xr$. And the solidity of both is $\frac{1}{3}x^2rl$. Hence the difference of the true pyramids and the average prisms is the differenee of $\frac{1}{3}$ and $\frac{1}{4}$ or $\frac{1}{12}x^2rl$.

262. *If there is a cross slope at one end, take the average depth of the right and left and middle cuttings at each end; and from this depth find the solidity, as if there were no cross slope.*

This rule only gives approximate results; but usually they are sufficiently correct for practice. If great accuracy is required, divide the figure into prisms, wedges, and pyramids, and find the contents of each by their appropriate rules.

LECTURE XXII.

MATERIALS.

263. *The principal materials used by the Engineer are stone, brick, mortar, wood and iron.*

These having different qualities, as to strength, cost, and durability will be considered separately.

264. *Good building stone should be large and tough, free, and not affected by the air, by cold, or by water.*

By being large and tough, their strength is increased; by being free, or easily broken by the hammer, the wall can be put up rapidly and cheaply; by being unharmed by the chemical agencies in the atmosphere, by the wearing and decomposing action of water, and by the freezing and expanding power of heat and cold, the structure is rendered durable.

265. *Marble, sand-stone, granite, limestone, and clay free-stone have most of these qualities.*

Marble has them all, and is besides susceptible of a fine polish and handsome.

Some granites are too soft and friable, by an excess of mica; in some, the mica is deficient and the rock becomes too hard to be worked easily; the presence of a sulphuret of iron sometimes permits the air to decompose and crumble it; but generally, granite makes a good building stone, especially when hornblende is an ingredient in it.

No better test of its qualities can be had than to examine the rocks, after they have been quarried for some years and notice the effects produced on them by time.

Sand-stones when well cemented so as to be tough, make an excellent building stone. Sometimes their grain is fine and their appearance handsome.

Limestone vary much in quality. Some become harder under the action of the weather, while others are decomposed and destroyed. Often they are hard, durable, easily quarried, free and regular, making a good building stone.

Clay is often largly mixed with lime, as a component in rocks, and the compound forms a good material for building. But clay alone as in the slates, is seldom strong and durable.

266. *In a wall of stone, the layers should be horizontal and the vertical joints should be broken.*

If the ground at the foundation is not level, it should be made so, or dug into horizontal steps. The courses of rock should not be made level by means of mortar, or small chippings of stone, but by having the upper and lower surfaces of the two rocks to fit each other.

When the bed of a rock is inclined, it tends to slide, and thus weakens the wall.

If the vertical joints are not broken by putting the middle of a rock over the joint in the row beneath it, the wall is rendered weak, liable to crack and yield under the weight above it.

267. *Bricks are made of a mixture of clay and sand, and when well made are very durable.*

These are used by the Engineer, when rocks are scarce, for aqueducts, locks, tunnel-arches and culverts.

The clay and sand should be in proper proportions and well mixed; carefully separated from the grit and small stones; well pressed in the mould; dried thoroughly, both under shelter and in the open air; burned slowly at first until the steam stops rising, and then heated just to a white heat for about 24 hours.

268. *Mortar is made with lime and sand and water, using about* 3 *bushels of sand to one of lime.*

The lime should be pure, with no clay in the stone from which it is burned; obtained from a hard carbonate, as marble, compact limestone, shells, and not from chalk or rotten limestone; quick or unslacked, until it is to be used; and sifted, to be clear of silex or unburnt stone.

The sand should be not rounded or worn but rough and sharp; neither fine or coarse; clean, free from clay, dirt, and vegetable mould; and not impregnated with salt, as it is usually when obtained on the sea-shore.

When the sand and lime have these qualities and are well mixed together with water, they *set* or harden well, forming a carbonate and silicate of lime, which becomes harder with time and clings firmly to the stone or brick.

If the lime is good and strong, 3 bushels of sand may be used with 1 of lime; 4 and even 7 if well mixed, have been tried with advantage to the strength of the mortar. With inferior lime 1 or 1½ bushels of sand are all that can be used. The mortar should be well moistened, especially in warm weather, so that the brick or stone should not absorb so much of the water as to leave a supply insufficient for the formation of the carbonate.

Walls should not be put up in winter, when the mortar might freeze before setting, as such mortar would never harden; nor should they be worked on in wet weather, as the rain would wash the mortar from the joints and also carry off some of the lime from the mortar.

269. *When mortar, made from common lime, can be well dried before it is exposed to water, it will suit for some works under water, but usually hydraulic lime must be obtained.*

This will harden under water in a very short time. The limestones from which this lime is obtained are not pure, but contain 40 or 50 per cent. of clay, sometimes clay and manganese, or clay and magnesia; a small quantity of silex or oxide of iron is frequently found in hydraulic limestones. When burnt they will not slack by air or water, but have to be pulverised by mechanical means. The best and most convenient test of the suitableness of any rock for making hydraulic lime, is the actual trying of the rock, and noticing how the mortar becomes hard under water.

The hydraulic lime is mixed with sand about in the same proportions as in common mortar. Formerly it was scarce and costly, but it has been found in more and more localities, uutil it is now nearly as cheap as common lime. This mortar is called cement, but for works out of water it is not as strong as common mortar. Thus, for a stone bridge, the cement would be used for the piers, but not for the arches which span the stream. Its only peculiarity is that it sets under water.

LECTURE XXIV.

MATERIALS CONTINUED.

270. *Wood is used for bridges, aqueducts and many other purposes by the American Engineer, when stone or iron would be employed in other countries.*

Its abundance and cheapness permit this, although it requires to be often renewed, while the stone or iron would last for ages. The great elasticity of wood, the ease with which it can be worked or shaped in any desirable form, its strength, toughness and lightness, make it as important to the Engineer as any of the materials he uses.

271. *Of the several kinds of wood, pine, chesnut, oak, and cypress, are most used by the Engineer.*

The abundance and cheapness of pine, its being soft and easily cut by the plane or axe, and its high degree of strength and durability, make it more used than all the other kinds of wood put together. The sap wood of the trunk is sometimes large, and this is of little value, since it decays very rapidly. When the tree is saturated with turpentine, the wood is almost indestructible by time, and suits admirably for many purposes of the Engineer.

White oak and post oak are much esteemed. Both are more durable than pine in exposed situations; both are stronger and tougher, but they are not as easily worked nor as cheap.

Chesnut is soft, and durable, not as strong as pine, but as the tree soon begins to rot at the heart, it is difficult to get large sound timbers or broad plank from it.

Cypress and cedar are mnch like chesnut, but more durable. The common black locust is hard, strong, and very durable. These are the most common woods, used by the Engineer, though for particular purposes and in some localities others are employed.

273. *The sap remaining in the wood is the principal or only cause of rot or decay.*

Woody fibre, well seasoned, will be perserved for ages when not exposed to moisture ; and under water, in certain conditions it is alike durable. The sap, containing a large proportion of albumen which is easily decomposed, begins to change itself and then propagates its changes into the wood. As yeast begins and extends a change in other substances, so the sap begins the transformation of the wood.

The proof of this consists in the slow decay of some woods in which the albumen is small, in those timbers where the sap is nearly or entirely removed, or when it is kept in a dry state incapable of chemical transformation, or where it is neutralised by the introduction of foreign chemical agents.

273. *The sap is farther injurious, by inviting the attacks of insects and the growth of fungi in the wood.*

It is sweet and also nourishing, while the woody fibre will not support animal life. The albumen, beginning to decompose, forms ammonia, and this favors the growth of a parasitic fungus, which strikes its roots deep into the substance of the wood and entirely destroys its texture.

274. *Lumber should be cut in winter or mid-summer, and not in spring or autumn.*

In the spring the sap rises faster than the small new leaves can elaborate it into wood-making sap ; and in the autumn the leaves beginning to decay, are again inefficient. In the midsummer, the leaves transform it as fast as it rises, and no accumulation takes place. In the winter, but little if any rises. As the rot is caused by the sap, the winter and midsummer, when this fluid does not abound in the tree, is the proper time for felling.

275. *The trees should be mature before felling ;* 20 *years being sufficient for chesnut,* 50 *for pine, and still more for oak.*

The young tree superabounds in sap-wood ; and its fibres are not so close and compact as when they are older. In the chesnut the time of reaching maturity is short, and the heart being older than the outer layers often begins to rot while the tree is growing with vigor.

276. *To preserve timber from rotting, it should be thoroughly seasoned, so as to remove the sap.*

This is best done by drying it in the open air. For pine a year is sufficient; for oak two or three are necessary, and longer if the pieces are thick. Oak should be seasoned under cover; but pine only needs shelter from the sun to prevent its cracking and warping.

In this operation the wood absorbs moisture, from the damp air, which dissolves the sap, and the mixture is then abstracted when the atmosphere becomes drier. This being often repeated most of the sap is removed.

If the timber is steeped in water for some time, either in the log or after being sawed, it will season afterwards very rapidly. In this case, the sap is displaced more or less by the water, which water is soon removed afterwards in the dry air, or a hot sun.

Seasoning is sometimes effected by kiln-drying. This is a more rapid process, being completed in a week or two, but it leaves much of the sap still in the wood in a dry state ready to become active when an opportunity is offered for the absorption of water.

Steaming the timber is another method of seasoning. This is a rapid and effective process, and if it could be done economically it would generally be introduced.

An expensive but effective method has been tried in England, in which the sap is removed by standing the timbers in a large cast-iron cylinder, from which the air is then exhausted. This causes the internal fluids to come out rapidly and the sap is thus removed. If when thus deprived of sap, the wood is placed in a solution of pyrolignite of iron, this substance is absorbed, and the iron deposited permanently in the cells, to the exclusion of moisture, so that the wood is well preserved against rotting.

Charring is sometimes resorted to for posts, not only to expel the sap, but to protect the surface of the part buried in the ground, by a layer of charcoal which will not decay. The advantages of this process are more or less doubtful.

280. *The rotting of timber is increased by its being kept wet and dry in succession; by the heat of warm climates; and by contact with decaying materials.*

If all the while dry it will last for ages. So if kept in water, especially in cool climates and running streams. But if successively wet and dry, it will rot rapidly. Posts, ground-sills, rail-road sills, decay very rapidly for this reason. Even for white oak or chesnut, the durability of rail-road timbers is not over six or eight years, and for pine not over five or six.

As heat favors chemical changes, and cold stops them entirely, timber will decay more rapidly in a southern than in a northern climate; while, far to the north, the winter does no injury at all to timber, however exposed.

If the rot begin at one part of a piece of wood, it is rapidly propagated to the rest; so if the timber is in contact or near other decaying pieces. So also if in pools or stagnant water, where vegetable matter is undergoing decomposition.

281. *Besides the common rot to which timber is exposed, it is subject to the dry rot in close moist places.*

This begins on the inside while the outside appears sound and dry. The whole mass becomes a mere powder, losing all its strength and elasticity. This rot, once begun, spreads with great rapidity, and is usually accompanied by a fungus growth whose branches penetrate the whole substance of the wood. It is likely to prevail in cellars, in the holds of ships, in the under timbers of a house, and generally in places where there is considerable moisture and no free circulation of the air.

It is to be prevented by thorough seasoning of the timber, by ventilating the confined places, and by cutting off the rotten parts when the decay has once begun.

282. *Both common and dry rot may be prevented by impregnating the timber with a solution of corrosive sublimate or of pyrolignite of iron.*

As no care in seasoning will abstract all the sap, its power to injure is destroyed, by combining it with salts, which form a permanent compound that can not be decomposed by water or air at ordinary temperatures.

Corrosive sublimate, which is a bi-chloride of mercury, will enter into a chemical union with the albumen of the sap and form a permanent compound with it. A solution is made containing one pound of this salt and 5, 10, or 15 gallons of water, and in this the timber is steeped 10 or 15 days.

This process was patented by Kyan in England in 1828, and is called Kyanising. It is approved by the best chemists of the age, and has been used extensively in England, and to some extent in this country with great success, for preserving rail-road timbers. The wood prepared in this way has been exposed to the severest tests without injury In 1838, upwards of 24 millions of feet of this Kyanised timber was laid down on the Great Western rail-road in England, and an official report was published in 1844, stating that no signs of rot had been discovered in a single piece, after an extensive examination of the track. Three rail-road Companies in New England have since this time Kyanised all their timbers, and the results have been satisfactory to the Engineers and to the Companies.

The cost of this preparation varies from 5 to 8 dollars per thousand feet of board measure, and may be used advantageously whenever the timber would decay in six or eight years, and when the labor and interruption of renewing would be considerable.

The pyrolignite of iron is a much cheaper preparation than corrosive sublimate. It was introduced by Boucherie of France and is extensively used there. But the experiments with this substance have not been so long continued and have not therefore inspired as much confidence as with Kyanised wood.

With both, the great difficulty consists in making the solution penetrate into all parts of the timber. To aid and accelerate this, they sometimes place the wood in a large close iron tank over which the solution is poured and then subjected to great hydraulic pressure. If the wood is green and fresh-cut, the sap vessels seem to aid the absorption, and the pressure is not so much needed.

Boucherie tried various methods to produce the necessary penetration. The tree yet standing was bored through, near the bottom of the trunk, and the solution confined around the tree by a water-tight bag. Or the trunk, soon after being felled, was made to stand in a tank containing the solution. A better method still was to invert the timbers so that the butt end was upwards, and confine the solution in a bag around the upper part. All these plans, though troublesome, were effective.

283. *The crude iron as it first comes from the furnace, being brittle, must be made tongh by hammering and rolling, before it is suitable for rails.*

These operations decarbonize the crude iron, and change very much its mechanical properties; but as they require fuel and labor, they increase its cost. This expense is, however, indispensable, as only wrought iron can be used for rails.

284. *Charcoal iron, or anthracite, is better than the coke iron; American is better than the English.*

The fuel used in reducing the ore has a great influence on the value of the iron. Charcoal does no injury; but the bituminous coal, or coke made from it, often contains sulphur, and sometimes other foreign elements which depreciate the iron very much. The anthracite coal is more pure and does less harm.

In the United States, charcoal is generally used in the furnace; sometimes anthracite; seldom bituminous coal. In England, most of the iron is made with coke, and is inferior to ours.

285. *Not less than five per cent. per annum should be estimated for deprecation in the English iron rail. For the American, it is decidedly less.*

Some rails break in the middle, and some separate into thin layers, thus losing all their tenacity; on others the projections at the upper part are crushed and torn off; all wear away and rust more or less. The tonnage on different roads, and the rapidity of the trains, and the weight of the engines, and the quality of the iron, will each influence the durability of the rail; but seldom will the average life even of the T pattern exceed 20 years. With good American iron their duration would be longer.

LECTURE XXV.

STATE IMPROVEMENTS.

286. *The usual organization for making a rail-road or canal is a chartered corporation.*

Individual capital being insufficient even for a short line, the union of many into one legal body, having unity of counsel, action, interest, and responsibility, is appropriate and necessary.

287. *No peculiar privileges or monopolies of any kind should be granted to these corporations, and all proper restraints should be imposed on their powers.*

They are united together for one object, the building of a road, because individuals cannot accomplish the object; every thing necessary for this end, and no more, should be given them.

They should have no exclusive right to build roads, no privilege of holding unnecessary real estate, no right to issue bank-bills, and no release from the ordinary obligations of capital to pay taxes for the support of the State.

The privilege of taking necessary land and materials, at a fair price, to be determined by a jury in case of disagreement as to their value, is indispensable to the corporation, and may be given with safety and propriety.

On the other hand, the Company should be held strictly to account, as common carriers; a maximum charge for goods by weight and by measure, and for passengers, should be fixed by their charter; a penalty for excessive charges should be imposed, and a simple, easy and cheap mode of enforcing this penalty should be prescribed.

Unless these and similar limitations should be provided in the charters of Rail Road Companies, their immense wealth and influence enable them to impose on private individuals and interfere with the natural course of trade and travel.

288. *Every charter asked for by individuals should be granted without expense or delay.*

As rail-roads promote the public good and are of immense advantage to the people, every refusal to grant a charter for a road is an injury done to the community, and an interference with the rights of the people. Every attempt to depress local interests for the gain of others, is an injustice not to be permitted in a free and republican country. Free trade and unlimited competition is right and just in rail-roads as in commerce. As common roads are always granted, when the damages done to private property are fairly paid for, so rail-roads should always be permitted, whenever capitalists can be found willing to construct them.

289. *Our State Governments make many blunders in undertaking the construction of rail-roads.*

The Legislature is not a proper judge of the propriety of building a rail-road along any particular route; they are not enough interested in the matter to examine it carefully; they are too much engrossed with other duties to decide on it correctly; they are biassed by sectional or private interests; they are influenced by the opinions of prominent political favorites who may have a bias or interest of their own in the result; and often it happens that however pure their motives, and however anxious to decide correctly, many of the members are unable to arrive at a proper conclusion.

When the work is once resolved on, the best line is not selected, unprofitable branches are added and new works projected, where none had before been thought of, in order to satisfy the clamors of opponents or to promote sectional or private interests.

In the construction of the work, every expenditure is increased by the frauds, the incompetency, and the negligence of the State's agents; high prices are paid to Engineers, managers, and contractors; jobs are given to party favorites; work is taken from the hands of contractors before it is fully finished; extra allowances are made for work really included in the contracts; the most costly mode of construction is adopted; double tracks are made, though not at all needed; the work is badly done, though extravagantly paid for; and care is not taken of the finished work, so that it soon needs repairs or renewal.

The changes of parties and of the people introduce new officers and superintendents, and these alter without improving the details of management, and thus increase the expenditure without any corresponding benefit. It often happens that a new Legislature is entirely opposed to the action of the first, so that the whole work is suspended and heavy damages paid to contractors for terminating their contracts; the suspension is however temporary, for a change of counsellors renews the abandoned work.

After the road is finished and brought into use, the tolls are adjusted to the clamors of the people, rather than to the best interests of the road; the superintendent and other officers, appointed with reference to party politics, are incompetent or inefficient; changes are continually introduced in the management, by the ups and downs of parties; the repairs of the track, the cars, and the engines, are not effected with economy; waste, extravagance and negligence accompany all the business of the road.

290. *The State can neither construct or manage a railroad as economically as a private company.*

The first cost of the road being more than if it were built by private capital, and the gross receipts being more largely reduced by expensive management, the net profits are lessened by two causes, both of the utmost importance.

The State of Georgia has constructed a road, 140 miles long, which has cost the State more than four millians of dollars, or if we include the interest on the outlay, about seven millions, while the road is yet laid in part with light iron and poorly supplied with engines and cars. From this immense expenditure the State Treasury is not receiving a single farthing, though it is hoped that after a while the road will begin to pay something.

The States of Pennsylvania, Indiana, Illinois and Michigan have expended millions on their public works; but the last three States have abandoned all at great loss to private Companies; while Pennsylvania is burdened with a heavy tax to pay the interest on her internal improvement debt.

New York had a fine opportunity to make a profitable investment in her Erie Canal; but by constructing other works which have been unproductive, and by spending large sums in widening and deepening her canal, and in doubling and enlarging its locks, the income does not now more than pay the interest on the whole cost.

No other State has constructed any works that have been profitable to them as stockholders.

291. *The State expenditures on rail-roads are almost always unjust to a portion of the State.*

The losses being paid by taxes on all the citizens, fall heavily on some sections of the State, where they have derived no advantage from the roads.

292. *Private enterprise will, in most cases, if not always, construct such works as are needed.*

Few States are better supplied with rail-roads than New Jersey and Connecticut, considering their size and population; yet all have been built by private capital. The rail-roads in New York have all been constructed in the same way, except the Erie road, and on that the State lost the whole of the three millions she subscribed. In Illinois and Indiana, private companies are covering the whole country with a magnificent net-work of rail ways, after the State had made a complete failure in similar undertakings. So likewise in other States.

293. *The magnitude of an enterprise does not require the intervention of the State.*

The Erie Rail Road wields a capital of over 20 millions;

the Reading Rail Road nearly as much; and few if any of the States should try their credit to this extent.

294. *The subscription by the State of a small part of the stock in a private company is liable to but few of these objections.*

Private capital being mainly employed, the vigilance of self-interest prevents waste, extravagance and mismanagement; the losses, if any, will be small; the individual benefit to a portion of the people being large, will be purchased at a small cost, that will readily be borne by the rest, who receive little or no advantage.

Were the subscription of the State larger than one-half or two thirds of the capital stock, the controlling influence of private interest would not be sufficient to save the State from mistakes and losses. Many individuals, whose interests would be benefited by the road, would subscribe for a portion of the stock, even if the road should be a poor investment.

The aid which has been afforded by Alabama, South Carolina and Massachusetts, to their rail-roads, has not been injurious or objectionable; that of Tennessee and Virginia has been too large.

295. *The subscription by counties and cities is less objectionable than by the State.*

The whole of a county or of a city, often receive benefit from a road, and their loss, if any, as stockholders, will be made up by their individual advantage. The subscription is not made without a thorough discussion and vote of the people who are responsible for the expenditure. More vigilance and economy may be expected from a county than from the whole State, for any losses from bad management touch them more immediately.

296. *When a State has once embarked in the construction of rail-roads, she ought to withdraw by selling stock to individuals at a fair market price.*

To attempt to sell the whole Road would involve a probable loss, since there would be but few competitors for so large a purchase. To sell stock would introduce the watchfulness of private interest, and secure prudence and economy in the management of the road. From half the stock in private hands, the State would probably receive larger dividends than from the whole of it under her own control.

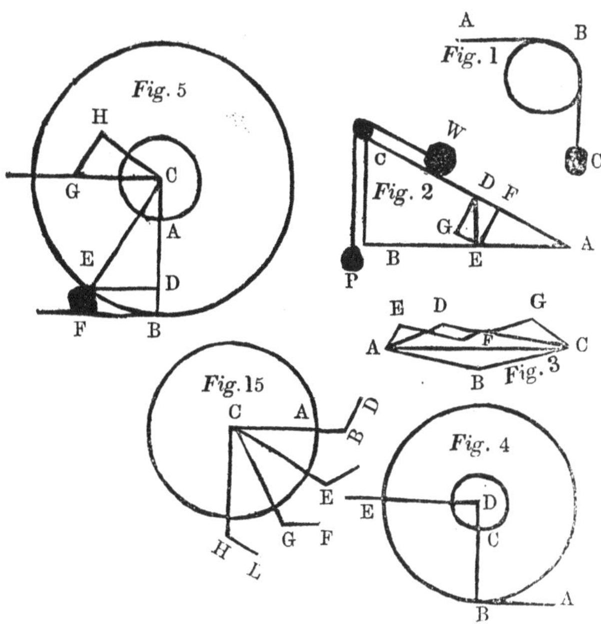
Fig. 5
Fig. 1
Fig. 2
Fig. 3
Fig. 15
Fig. 4

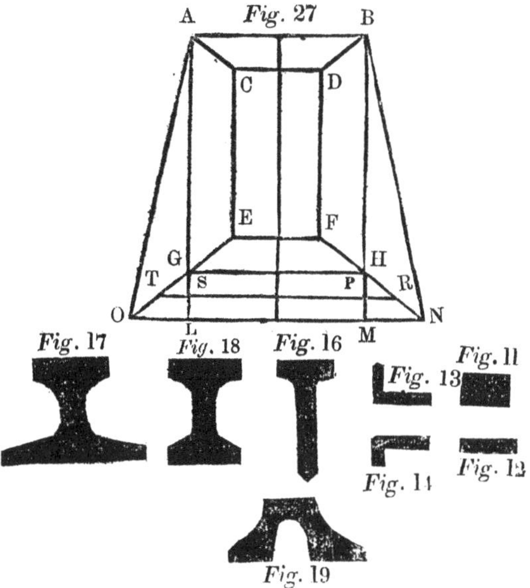
Fig. 27
Fig. 17
Fig. 18
Fig. 16
Fig. 13
Fig. 11
Fig. 14
Fig. 12
Fig. 19

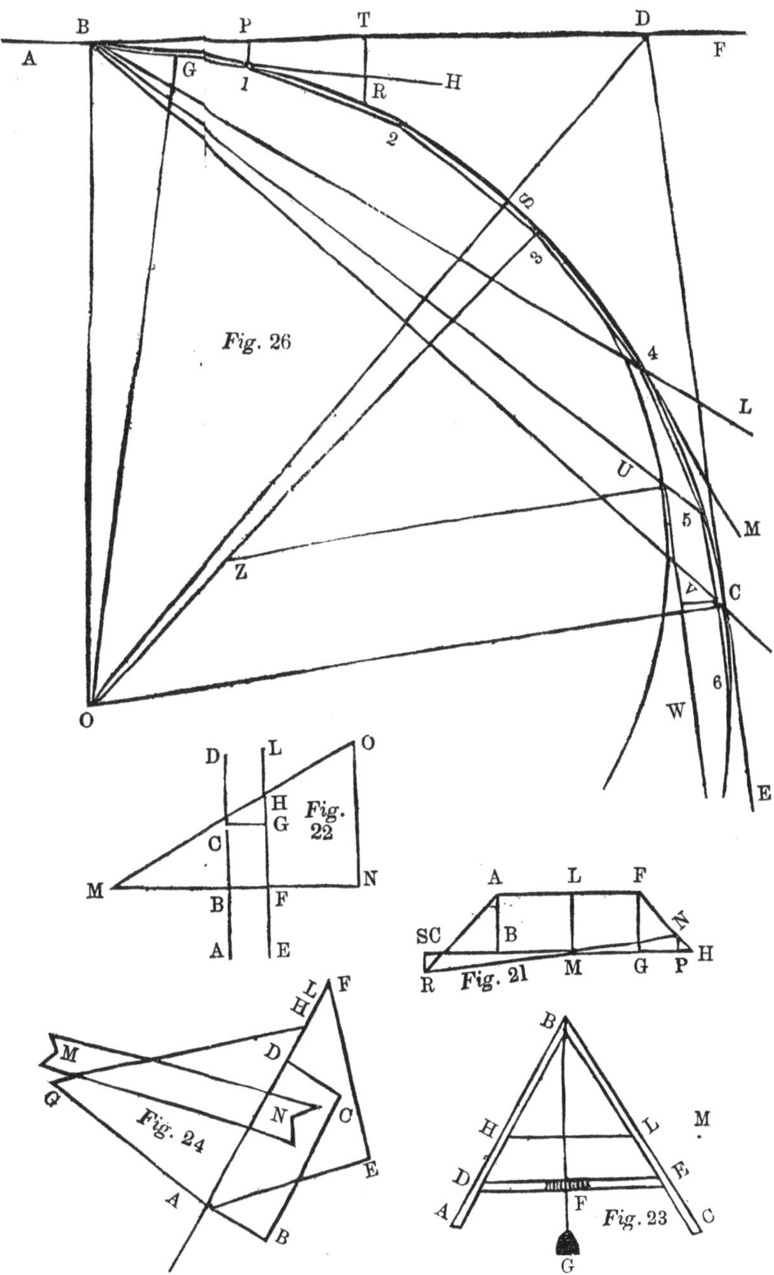

Fig. 26
Fig. 22
Fig. 21
Fig. 24
Fig. 23

www.ingramcontent.com/pod-product-compliance
Lightning Source LLC
LaVergne TN
LVHW021414110826
845150LV00007B/1925

* 9 7 8 1 4 2 5 5 1 1 7 2 2 *